A
GENESIS
IN MY BED

STEVE HACKETT
AUTOBIOGRAPHY

A
GENESIS
IN MY BED

STEVE HACKETT
AUTOBIOGRAPHY

WYMER
PUBLISHING
Bedford, England

First published in Great Britain in 2020
by Wymer Publishing
www.wymerpublishing.co.uk
Tel: 01234 326691
Wymer Publishing is a trading name of Wymer (UK) Ltd

ISBN: 978-1-912782-62-8

Front cover image Jo Hackett
Back cover image Armando Gallo
Typeset by Andy Bishop / 1016 Sarpsborg.
Printed by Clays, Bungay, Suffolk
A catalogue record for this book is available from the British Library.

To my lovely wife Jo,
mum June, dad Peter & brother John,
the whole family
and world of great friends

These are the Voyages of an Explorer

To boldly go unearthing snapshots

Of a myopic life form on the edge

Of an uncharted galaxy.

In short...

me

Contents

1

We're all toys of time...

Ducks were flying up walls, dish cloths and wallpaper shared the same murky colours and the smell of over-boiled sprouts wafted through stairwells throughout London. Its stoic inhabitants endured life through chilled smog. Like an interminable black and white episode of *Coronation Street*, the drab early fifties still featured food rationing whilst Britain was in the grip of a severe post-war depression. My parents' grim South London flat in Tradescant Road looked remarkably similar to the one the hapless young couple moved to in Richard Attenborough's film *10 Rillington Place*.

In the midst of this stifling environment I arrived, a fully-fledged red-faced screamer. I was a struggler from the start. To my parents' great delight, I wailed all night for the whole of the first year of my life. The only way I could deal with crib fever was by becoming an early head-banger. My mother insists that I was already standing up in my cot at six months in a failed bid to do a runner as I was clearly not content to merely dribble all over my manky toy Larry the Lamb.

Once I'd graduated from the cot any dreams of world domination had to be shelved until I'd mastered the art of climbing stairs instead of tumbling to the bottom.

Within a year or two I developed a tendency to wander off, particularly on the dreaded rainy shopping expeditions to Brixton. Whenever someone had forgotten to thoroughly nail me to my push chair, I made my escape. Imagine being a small child in the film *Blade Runner*... longing for trees, a patch of grass, or a view of the seaside, half remembered from an old children's picture book. That's what it was like for me in that world of pungent smells, oily puddles, dead cats in troughs, heavy duty tobacco pipes and cigarettes, swirling mist and chimney stacks belching black smoke... On one occasion I let go of my grandmother's hand when a bright tiger picture book cover in a shop window attracted my attention. Nanny couldn't find me anywhere and was naturally furious by the time I eventually emerged through the fog and milling crowds. Toddling off into the blue was a particular speciality of mine. Even today Mum refers to the constant problem of my early disappearances.

Thanks to Mum and Dad, my burgeoning wanderlust was taken on to a whole new level by the arrival of a fabulous gift called the *Gresham Flyer*.

One night as I was dreaming about a natty pair of dark glasses just beyond my reach, I found myself rudely awakened, then hauled, protesting loudly into the living room. Nothing had prepared me for the great surprise that was to follow. My complaints stopped mid-air as I caught sight of a shining red contraption on to which I was quickly hoisted. As my feet touched the pedals of my first tricycle it slowly began to move. Nothing in my three-year-old life had so far matched the excitement of that moment. If you'd offered me a trip to personally investigate the rings of Saturn in my own spaceship it couldn't possibly have competed with that thrill. I realise that when you don't have much, even as a child you really appreciate special things when they come your way, and certainly I did. Dad had bought it second-hand in Peckham and struggled back on foot with it for miles. He knew what it would mean to me. Peckham market sold everything, from stuffed aardvarks to exotic pets like snakes, crocodiles and monkeys. It hurts to think of all those poor creatures, trapped with little hope of survival. A world that had barely moved on since the time of Dickens. Of course, as a constant accident waiting to happen, I tried to touch a monkey through the bars of the cage and naturally, he bit me.

I realise I was not an easy child. I only had to look at a plug and it fell apart. I had the kind of mind that could take apart an alarm clock perfectly and then attempt to turn it into something else, by which point it was broken beyond repair. Mum says I was constantly trying to force large things into tiny spaces with a high degree of desperation... "Too mall, too mall!" Nothing I did was logical. The impossible had to be possible! It was just slightly out of my reach, that's all.

Mum had the tougher job of keeping an overactive, volatile toddler in line whilst Dad was out at work. Fathers often have it easier. Mine rarely admonished me but had to do a tap dance between politician and saviour when mother's patience was stretched to her wit's end. In my early days of playing one of them against the other, Dad was the softer touch. I guess all kids end up unwittingly putting their parents through hell. It's all part of growing up. My parents were practically kids themselves when I emerged. Mum only nineteen and Dad all of twenty-two.

For Mum, who'd not had an easy childhood throughout the lean and tough war years and had only just begun to have a taste of freedom with dances and parties, my appearance put pay to her social life.

Moreover, during those hard times money was

3

scarce for a newly wed couple. Every day was a struggle for them, and here was Screaming Beastie in tow. Being on the front line most of the time, Mum found it particularly difficult to cope. She'd lose her temper as my cries reached the decibels of a Marshall amp cranked up to 11... There'd be a massive explosion as the two of us collided like the irresistible force meeting the immoveable object. Finally, I'd be scooped up for a tearful reconciliation. Mum and I had a tough start, both of us out of step with the brown and grey smoke-stained compromised world constantly closing in on us.

Despite the hardships, Mum was stunningly beautiful. She had raven-haired olive-skinned looks that reflected her vibrant personality. Throughout my school years many of my young friends not only assumed she was my sister but often asked if I could arrange a date with her. If I'd had more of an entrepreneurial streak I could have sold tickets that would have stretched around the block, just to meet her.

By contrast, most of the mums who showed up at the school gates looked like they were determined to put off the merest hint of an advance from the entire male population. They sported overalls, scarves around their hair rollers and often coughed out orders with cigarettes dangling from the corners of their mouths.

One day I expressed my growing concern to Dad that Mum just wasn't like a 'normal' mum, to which he replied, "You don't want one of *those* do you? Aren't you happy that *your* mum is young and beautiful?" Thus reassured, I began to realise that it wasn't necessarily best to be one of the crowd.

Mother June was beautiful even as a child, but she did not have a particularly glamorous childhood, growing up in an even darker and grimier London, where some kids didn't even have shoes and many streets had to share one toilet. The smog was so bad you could not see beyond your outstretched arm. Mum had an especially tough time in the war years, sleeping underground in the tube when the air raids were on. Then she and her younger sister Betty were both evacuated away from home. Neither of them understood the necessity, but their mother Lillian did. She was an indomitable character who survived two world wars, (according to Mum she also started a few herself) and lived to the age of ninety-seven.

Lillian was naturally concerned, as bombing was heavy around their vulnerable Camden home. Evacuees weren't always treated fairly. Mum recollects adults stealing sweet rations for their own kids. Never one to suffer put-downs for long though, her positive spirits always kicked in, and all the boys had a hard time concentrating on their lessons once she showed up.

When Mum was seventeen, decked out in her finest, Dad spotted her at a dance. Dad, Peter, must have done a passable impression of Fred Astaire. He also had great soldier boy looks to rival a young Gregory Peck, as a paratrooper photo shows. At the end of the war he was drafted into the army and sent to Palestine as part of its beleaguered peace-keeping force. His training had involved seven or eight parachute jumps, two of which had to be undertaken in the pitch dark. Landing was reckoned to have the equivalent impact of jumping off a twelve-foot wall. Many youngsters didn't even survive the training. Their superiors were even allowed a ten percent casualty rate. During one night-jump Dad couldn't figure out which way up the ground was and landed on his head, immediately stunned, but protected by a helmet. Fortunately, quick wits saved him and he freed himself before being dragged through barbed wire.

I can see how Mum and Dad were attracted to each other. Between them, it was all parachutes and petticoats. Apart from his looks, he was a multi-faceted character with a 'Mensa' qualifying IQ rating, brilliant at football and cricket, a great talent for painting, and the ability to coax a tune out of most musical instruments, including bugle, clarinet, guitar and the all-important mouth organ.

I seem to hail from a long line of harmonica players as Ted (Mum's dad) also played the instrument. On Ted's side of the family as well as grandma Lillian's there came a whole tribe of musicians, including drummers, brass players and pianists with the odd music hall artiste. Ted's sister Saxon Davis the comedienne performed a risqué act dressed up as a girl guide singing a song entitled 'Gertie the Pride of the Guides'. As the pièce de la resistance, she hoisted up her skirt and proudly displayed her bloomers. Although Ted was a chauffeur for most of his working life, often for a titled 'Lady' heroin addict, showbiz was clearly in his blood and with his wicked sense of humour he really could have been a music hall turn as well.

Several of Ted's relations lived to a very old age, such as my Great Uncle Jack who reached 108 as the oldest living ex-service man from World War I. They were great survivors against the odds.

Ted's side of the family had a long bloody trail of tears. Originally from Poland, his Jewish ancestors managed to escape the Pogroms by the skin of their teeth. Ted's mother Rose recounted stories of women dragged along by their hair. They escaped via Portugal, where they were re-named Da Costa (people of the coast). Finally, in the UK they were given the name Davis, as part of a swift drive to integrate them into the East End community.

Lillian *also* had Polish ancestors who escaped

6

persecution, along with Irish ancestors who braved it across the sea, determined to feed their starving families. Dad's mother suffered on a more personal level. Aged fifteen, she ran away from North Wales, determined to escape an overbearing stepmother.

All my ancestors were drawn to London through hardship, seeking a place where a man could earn a crust knowing his family was no longer under the threat of total extinction. They were drawn into a dark, chaotic city where streets were paved with dung, sweat and grime rather than gold. They continued to fight for survival through the two world wars. Dad's father Jim insisted that service under fire was nothing compared to the horrors of the Blitz which reduced much of London to rubble. He heroically saved lives from many a blazing inferno during those sleepless nights.

1953 was a watershed year for my parents. They felt they'd hit the jackpot, moving from a cramped South London flat into the newly built Churchill Gardens housing estate in Pimlico, which replaced large tracts of bomb damage alongside the Thames.

Our block was named 'Sullivan' House whilst its neighbour was 'Gilbert'. Gilbert and Sullivan could have been a firm of toilet seat manufacturers for all I knew. I still can't forget my mother's joy on hearing that the flat had the luxury of hot running water and under-floor central heating. "You mean you could take baths all day long here?" She asked incredulously.

Clement Atlee's post war government had transformed Britain by modernising much of its housing and services enabling families such as ours to enjoy a higher standard of living. Broadly speaking, Churchill's team had won the war, but Atlee's rebuilt the country. The National

Health Service was newly born. The Welfare State was now up and running along with the hot water.

The optimistic mood of the post war era was celebrated with 1951's Festival of Britain. At the birth of London's Arts complex on the South Bank the Festival Hall opened on 4th May with all due pomp. Newsreel commentaries shown in all cinemas before the main feature reported the event in the following style... "Workers and housewives throughout the land are so happy to down tools and leave behind their lathes and scrubbing brushes to join that throng of loyal subjects lucky enough to catch a glimpse of King George and the ever glamorous Queen Elizabeth auguring in the new era of joy and plenty. It's not often that common folk get to have such a jamboree..." implying they should think themselves jolly well lucky to get any days off at all!

It took several years for the positive changes to effectively push through. Scars of the recent past were all too apparent. I grew up in a world of shell-shocked streets with dangerously unstable buildings. Even once we relocated to the relatively upmarket Pimlico in 1953, its once proud Georgian terraces which today have regained their former grandeur, had at that time been rocked to their very foundations by heavy bombing. The Luftwaffe had obviously done its job extremely well. Crumbling pillars adorned sad facades, appearing ripe for slum clearance. Together those houses resembled rows of rotting teeth with the odd gaping black hole of a bombsite to completely ruin any semblance of a smile. Although as kids we were naturally forbidden to play on those precarious sites, we couldn't figure out why, as they seemed irresistible. They beckoned our adventurous spirits. Two films I thought captured the excitement I remember of kids playing on London bombsites, were John Boorman's

Hope and Glory and Julian Temple's *Absolute Beginners*. Julian's film really does give a convincing picture of 1950s Pimlico with cheeky little sods up to no good at every turn.

The early 1950s provided us with a stodgy diet of light entertainment. Characters had time to smoke pipes and ponder in 'action' films of the fifties, the comfortable world of heroes in slippers served by compliant wives in aprons. 'Auntie' BBC was still tightly restricted by custodians who kept 'pop' music firmly in its place for half an hour on a Friday night if you were lucky.

There was only one real target audience, the family at home, where through a haze of cigarette smoke with the additional pong of overcooked meat and veg, fake coal fires and standard lamps stood sentinel. Programmes were weighed down with standard issue titles such as *Workers' Playtime, Woman's Hour* and the simply thrilling *Housewives' Choice.*

On *Two Way Family Favourites* we'd hear "From Bill and Mable and little Bobby to Uncle Humphrey and all his mates at BFPO 13", leaving you guessing unless you were 'in the know' where the bloody hell this remote military outpost was. The era that had inspired George Orwell's *1984* still had its tentacles firmly wrapped around the wireless and wasn't going to let go without a fight.

My early impressions were formed during an era that had yet to define itself. Although radio and TV would soon be warping the minds of wayward teens the world over, Elvis had not yet been invented. Even so, the available music crackling out of the wireless threw a lifeline to me. Mario Lanza was the reigning Monarch of Song and what a sound Lanza had! A voice to set ironing boards and teacups rattling throughout the land with the power of his high resonating notes. I used to roll around the floor in ecstasy at his vibrant 'Drinking Song' from *The Student Prince*. Frank Sinatra was still crooning 'Walking My Baby Back Home', a song that perplexed me as a child and I couldn't figure out how Frank had a newly formed 'baby' that could already walk...

Yet even in that rigid time of bowler hats and cloth caps, by 1955 you could hear Bill Haley's 'Rock Around The Clock', alongside 'The Blue Danube' and Glenn Miller's 'In The Mood' on the same programme. Rock 'n' Roll was to ring the changes and barricades were about to come down. Life was soon to ease up for a generation of downtrodden skivvies. Mangle and basin were to begrudgingly make way for the all-important washing machine.

I was poised for change from the second I was out of my cot and my young spirit was always at the ready to rebel. With the arrival of Rock 'n' Roll there was a new sense of excitement in the air. Music always seemed to be the key to my need for expression. The point of my crucial musical breakthrough made me feel the world could be re-born anew. It was never enough for me to just be on the outside listening in — I always wanted to be in there, making my own noise!

From age two when Dad brought home my first harmonica, I wanted to create music myself. I knew I was holding something special in my hands. I spent hours getting the feel of single notes. It was a magical feeling to be able to create my own sounds, to actually be the piper of the dance.

The brown and grey world around me evaporated as the colours of musical notes took over. Mum has always said I would take my harmonica out of its little case on the London Underground and attempt to play a tune that consisted of two notes over and over again. The great seriousness of this exercise apparently had many of the other passengers in stitches. I think I was intent on trying to isolate individual notes, to feel their vibration and tone, where most kids would be content to make a swift din before moving on to the next big thing.

There are certain key moments in life when those two inner contestants, observer versus participant, temporarily cease hostilities and in the space of a split second instantly find themselves in partnership. You're up against the wall. You can climb over it but never go back. You no longer have the luxury of staying out of the game. The road to inaction is closed forever. You've been given a gift. The wrapping paper is already discarded on the floor. Before you've realised it, you've become the thing you were always meant to be. Here's the first time it happened for me.

One day when I'd reached four years old, I was watching myself in Mother's dressing table mirror. Mum would have to sit to see herself properly, but at three feet high I could stand and see the whole picture. It was definitely a "Look mum, I can now do this!" moment. I was playing away on the mouth organ, just pretending, when suddenly I realised that I could manage several of the tunes I'd heard my father play.

It was a revelation. Out came plausible renditions of 'Scotland the Brave', 'God Save the Queen' and 'Oh Susanna'. In my mind I was onstage, giving my all to an audience of one — my mother. Other tunes were now to come flooding in... a liberal sprinkling of cowboy songs such as 'The Yellow Rose of Texas' became part of my pint-sized repertoire.

My early harmonicas had missing notes. 'Push-button' versions (Chromatic) I was assured had all of them. I nagged Dad endlessly about getting the harmonica player's equivalent of a baby grand piano. "Do you think you'll be able to handle one?" he asked. To this day I feel the guilt of telling him that I'd already tried one, owned by the father of a friend. This was a complete fabrication, but sure enough one Christmas Eve when I awoke at three in the morning I delved into my presents at the end of my bed and found a silver and red Koch chromatic model. I put the thing to my lips blowing very quietly. Once I'd confirmed I now had all the missing notes I craved I put the little beauty away and slept soundly. I'd ignored ALL my other presents.

Not long after, on a good day, I could do a decent impression of one of my early harmonica heroes, Tommy Reilly, imitating him playing the *Dixon of Dock Green* series theme tune, which all serious warblers realise is mighty difficult as it's full of sharps and flats.

To this day Bob Dylan's exuberant sounds on the 'harp', which always produce such a hearty cheer from stadium audiences throughout the world, owes everything to the child's joy of making the instrument emit as much noise as possible, practically at random.

Squeeze boxes around the campfire, cowboys and Indians and "You're my prisoner" at full tilt. Clever Bob has a skip and a jump in his mouth organ moves. It's one of the reasons why we love him — that early connection to child's play. It always reminded me of my love of the harp, awakened in childhood.

But the tentacles of the grey world around me were constantly poised and at the ready. My fondness for roaming the streets from an early age was often thwarted in my pre-school years by other kids, sometimes encouraging me into trouble, other times challenging or threatening. You'd think it was only boys, but some of the worst bullies were girls several years my senior who went around in a gang.

At age four I was very small, and they appeared huge to me as they joined forces to close in. Spearheaded by a ringleader called Christine, this tribe of Amazons would surround me and shove me around. On one occasion, I felt they were closing in for the kill, pushing and hitting me. I must have screamed out as I was terrified. Suddenly, a large hand appeared in their midst. They seemed to evaporate back into the mist as I was removed from the scene. My saviour was my dad… If he was nearby, he'd come to my rescue.

My first school was nightmarish. The teacher had no patience with kids, she wouldn't even let us go to the toilet and punishments were meted out regularly. I was terrified of her. Everything was harsh. No room for the imagination. Regimentation was the name of the day. We were taught to repeat the Lord's Prayer until we had all memorised it perfectly. We were also told it was even better to say it to yourself at bedtime! When I tried that out just before descending into the Land of Nod, I dreamed of the Wicked Witch of the West from *The Wizard of Oz*. There she was with that terrible green face grimacing at me as she dipped her broom in a bucket of water and scrubbed my face with it. Naturally I woke in some considerable distress. Don't laugh… She terrified me as she had done when I first saw the film. Over time I came to regard the film with affection, which is more than can be said for religion, which I always mistrusted from that scary night onwards. I felt God had let me down. He was obviously in league with the witch...

School at this time was one of the worst experiences of my life, in fact so bad that my parents decided to remove me from the place. The next school was better… but 1950s England was full of horrendous establishments and soon after another nightmare presented itself…

The doctor advised my parents that I should be sent to a convalescence home because of my constant sneezing and wheezing. On arrival my precious harmonica was taken away, along with some chocolates I had. It was like arriving at a Victorian workhouse. The tall red brick building had clearly not changed since the nineteenth century and neither had its workforce. We were shown to our beds in a spartan dormitory and then ushered downstairs to the dining area where they immediately gave us salad, which to this day I can't eat.

My parents had gone home leaving me alone in this black hole of Calcutta. What had I done to deserve this? When I really acted up as a child Mum threatened to send me to a home. The sheer terror of this prospect generally made me cooperate. It seemed to me that moment I had always dreaded had now arrived. My confidence had already been slashed by the bad start at school. Now in this Godforsaken institution I felt catapulted back into another cold world where love had no place, and even more so because I couldn't go home at night.

What had I done wrong? My brother John had just been born, and I was sad to be apart from him too. Far from feeling jealous, I felt protective towards him and I loved his little hands. I badly missed baby John, as well as my parents.

This place was in Broadstairs. It might just as well have been Broadmoor! Every day you had to line up for a large spoon full of castor oil, like some scene out of *Oliver Twist*. When I said I didn't eat salad in the refectory they forced me to sit there until I'd finished it and told me "If you don't finish it, he sees"... Following the pointed finger, I looked up at a grim face staring back at me from a painting on the wall. The eyes seemed to pierce through me. I was now convinced the place was haunted and I was frightened every night in the large dark dormitory where shadows seemed to morph, grow and approach the bed...

14

The mornings offered little respite. One day blurred into another. We were often stuck in a room with little to do. Occasionally they would read to us. The book I remember most was *Alice in Wonderland*. After repeatedly hearing "off with their heads!" I believed that I was going to be killed. I wondered which of the cold faces around me would do the deed.

They wouldn't let parents visit for at least two or three weeks. I thought this was it... I'd been abandoned and here was the home I'd always dreaded. I spent hours alone, trapped with the terrors of my imagination. There was only one kind woman there. She was known as staff nurse. I misinterpreted this as "star nurse". She was the only one who was nice to me. She was my equivalent of the Blue Fairy in the *Pinocchio* story. I fell in love with her kind smile. She was the only sweetness there... a light I held on to until my eventual release at the end of the summer holiday.

That dark place was like a scene out of a Charles Dickens novel. In fact, Dickens wrote *David Copperfield* in Broadstairs, and many consider that *Bleak House* was based on the place where he stayed there. Maybe the sea air helped my lungs a bit, but I've always had that weakness. It was probably the fault of Battersea Power Station, which continuously belched out sulphurous fumes, sometimes enveloping the whole of London in a kind of fog Jack the Ripper could have used to go about his business in broad daylight if he'd been stalking the streets in the twentieth century.

It came into my dreams... Before me as I flew up between the giant smokestacks, appeared a flying pink pig. "This will one day make a perfect album cover", I thought...

Okay I joke, but there is a nugget of truth in this. What was to become Pink Floyd's iconic album cover image, that great monolithic cloud factory *was* directly opposite my bedroom window at Sullivan House. I stared at it with five-year-old eyes… There it was, a gigantic four-mouthed monolith standing as sentinel of the city, like the multi-headed hound Cerberus guarding the entrance to the ancient Greek underworld.

The columns rising from the smokestacks seemed to create the ash grey sky above me... There was no separation between the two. I often watched the purring monster and marvelled at how its pipe dreams of clouds appeared to spread out to cover the whole of London. With the innocent perception of a child I could only sense that it held the keys to a paradox. The city had made a devil's pact with this monster, which gave us all warmth and light whilst at the same time polluting us with its poisonous breath. Here was an art deco monument to the days that gave rise to exciting new advances in technology, yet also to horrors like Hitler's Germany with similar towering chimneys that belched out the darkest of secrets. Although this beast has long since been put to sleep, its carcass still stands like a temple, a monument to a bygone industrial age, its huge image reflected in the swirling depths beneath.

The river always held a fascination, especially at night when the sounds of huge coal barges merged with noises of other river traffic groaning and hooting. In the dark the water was awash with snaking colours from bright neon signs. It teamed with activity, even while we slept. My old Genesis mates talk about their childhood country idylls, but for me the sounds of the Thames still hold an unparalleled magic... that strangely vibrant pulse of life, constantly beating in the midst of all the stress and hardship.

In later years I often tried to re-create the atmosphere of those times, repopulating that lost world in song.

As Father Thames lies sleeping
His ever watchful sons…

But the mercurial riverside held a new surprise for me…

Although Mother Earth was submerged beneath the decaying old world, with its smog, dirt, bustling markets, pungent smells and the concrete of Pimlico, just over the water lay the centre of the child's dreaming universe… Battersea Park, which contrasted powerfully with the grim surroundings of drab, post war London, was our surrogate Summer Palace garden and stood alone in technicolour just fifteen minutes skipping distance away from home, across Chelsea Bridge from one world to another.

The park was large, verdant and full of wonders. It contained a miniature steam railway, a boating lake, dancing fountains, deer and a zoo, but most importantly London's only permanent funfair.

I can recall the first time aged four when I experienced it all. From my first visit life was never the same. Imagine the sunniest day you'd ever seen. I was breathing something far richer than mere oxygen.

Everything here had been designed to thrill. The park was full of wonders. It was a beautiful day and the thing I remember was noises mingling with intoxicating smells of freshly made donuts, toffee apples along with clouds of pink candyfloss. The golden mile lined with kiosks was a seemingly endless outpouring of music, laughter and excitement… In short, a visit to heaven, all before reaching what became the nerve centre of my dreaming universe, Battersea Funfair itself.

Armed with a ferocious new cap gun and lasso I was determined to explore… I was taken on this thing called the tree walk. I assumed this was constructed by the ingenious elves that peered out from the trunks and branches, tantalisingly just out of reach. It was a lovely idea that you could walk up to a platform that ran between several trees. It seemed so inventive, as if Toyland was up there! I was visiting a world where gravity had been suspended in a universe of huge toys, some of which you could ride. Little boats punted around on a lake, powered by diesel, the strong smell of which put me on a high. At the park entrance was a model railway, its tiny green engine spluttering and clanking as realistically as its full-sized counterparts that steamed in and out of Victoria Station.

Nearby was something I found particularly scary and the source of the odd nightmare. It was called the grotto. This dark place that was made to look like a cave terrified me as a kid and it was significant in terms of confronting early childhood fears. At the entrance were earth-coloured busts of the four winds set into alcoves. They had what looked like gargoyle grimaces and seemed almost human, but plausibly like Egyptian mummies or ghosts of the dead. The chilling sound of rushing air like a moaning wind came from within the alcoves. The same noise as when you put a seashell to your ear, it filled the interior of this cave. It was as if you were passing into the very entrance to Hades itself!

So, it freaked the life out of me when adults tried to take me down there as a small child. The first time didn't work. I reached out my hand and asked to be picked up. When this didn't work, I went into one of my classic early performances, which resembled a total nervous breakdown. My body went rigid, then jack-knifed backwards. Tears in full flow, I howled like feedback from an overloaded fuzz box and was swiftly removed for the sake of world peace. Eventually I agreed to be taken through by one of Mum's friends on the condition that I could bury my face in her shoulder. But I peeped out every now and again.

First, we were walking on a narrow metal bridge over a live volcano, a large kind of glowing fire effect, which seemed real enough. I was pleased to have survived that, so I continued to take glances as we descended a spiral staircase into a far less creepy zone. A fountain appeared. It looked like coloured water in a gently pulsating subterranean cavern that shimmered with a phosphorescent glow. Finally, we walked over shingle as we passed these day-glow light mirrors, with ultra-violet strip-lighting which meant that if you were wearing white you shone as part of the show. I remember I congratulated myself when I finally reached the end of the grotto, no longer fearful and feeling as if I'd braved hell itself to reach a rainbow-hued marvel.

Just beyond the Grotto was the entrance to Battersea Funfair, a riot of colour and magic, but also a place where many frightening challenges had to be overcome. It took a few years for me to brave the perils of the Water Chute and Ghost Train. But then there were genuinely dangerous things like the Big Dipper roller coaster that eventually was to cause a major accident, killing several people through a derailment. There was also the terrifying Ball of Death. This involved motorbikes inside a metal ball. Often there were two being ridden at the same time. One would be going around the perimeter of the thing, while the other was moving from bottom to top. It's extraordinary that it was even humanly possible to perform such a feat.

One particularly challenging ride in the fairground was the Rotor, which I enjoyed as an older child. I spent endless time on it. I remember being stuck to the wall of this huge cylinder spinning with a G-force that held you and up to thirty others up against the side. You'd be standing there. It would move faster and faster… You'd be pulled closer and closer to the wall. Eventually the floor would move away, and you'd feel like you were laying down, but not with the normal force of gravity. The G-force was much stronger. You were like a fly on the wall stuck on this thing. It made you feel very uncomfortable, but just felt like it had to be gone through, as in some kind of rite of passage to show that you were tough. There were guys who were able to walk around on it. I tried to do that, but the pull of it was immensely strong and I could only kneel on it. These real hard men could get right up to the top and stand upright! I'm sure those rockers pulled plenty of girls doing that sort of stuff! It was your sort of heroic greaser that seemed to operate a lot of these rides... the rock 'n' roll tubs, the waltzers, the bumper cars. Unfortunately, I went on it so many times in succession that eventually I threw up, which cured me forever of that thing!

Outside the Rotor on the wall were pictures of girls with their skirts having ridden up. Whenever that happened, they always seemed shocked, but I guess that was half the fun! Propriety was maintained at an absolute minimum at the funfair. Carousels cantered away from the distant banshee wail of the Ghost Train, while the smell of diesel oil and burnt rubber cut through blurred arcs of coloured lights spilling their paint onto the night sky as the whole place pitched and tossed like a tattered sail ship in a typhoon.

The colourful fairground was a great escape from the oppressive grey of Pimlico. The funfair is now long gone and the only way back is in song. Memory of the fair is music to my ears...

As the wheel's turning a film starts to play
Of all the ones who just got away

2

Take a trip, take a ride through Darktown...

I always yearned for one form of escape or another, but knowing I'd be sucked back into the grey world surrounding me. The funfair gave brief moments of excitement, but exotic places were a distant dream way beyond my reach, until one day a real adventure unexpectedly presented itself... We were about to emigrate to Canada. Mum and Dad had decided...

Aunts, uncles, family friends, everyone seemed to be doing it. The whole world couldn't be wrong, could they?

We boarded the *Homeric* at Dover... Mum, yours truly and baby John. I was all of seven, John two. It hadn't dawned on me that this was planned as a journey from which there would be no return. Well-wishing aunts, Margaret and Barbara, were briefly allowed aboard to see us off.

The decision to fully embrace the New World was finally brought home to me when Auntie Margaret botched her warm goodbyes by suddenly bursting into tears. I hadn't realised how strong her feelings were until that moment. In the way that children are prone to switch loyalties at the drop of a hat, her vulnerability instantly conferred on Margaret a new title, the Most Beautiful Girl in the World.

21

She'd snatched the crown from her younger sisters in one fell swoop. I no longer pondered from the available clutch of young maiden aunts, "who is the fairest of them all?" It now struck me for the first time there was a beauty that wasn't just skin deep. Despite all my magnificent efforts to the contrary, I was growing up.

Dad had already gone ahead some months earlier to get a job, a home and prepare Vancouver for the next British invasion.

This time my wanderings were filled with joy and fascination. Whilst I explored the ship, it soon became clear that I'd been let loose in a gleaming self-contained city that just happened to float. They seemed to have thought of everything. Dining rooms, dance floors and bars. On deck an open-air salt-water swimming pool, a full-sized indoor cinema, children's nursery and luxury cabins for all. The massive 26,000 tonne *Homeric* had been built in Panama during the last gasp of the golden age of travel.

Our Atlantic crossing lasted five days. I regaled passengers and crew with mouth organ favourites (whether they wanted it or not). Well-intentioned but ultimately useless showers of change, mainly sixpences, found their way into my sweaty little hands.

I explored every part of the ship, even the labyrinthine engine rooms, when I wasn't chased off by the irate crew. One lost afternoon I skittled into the cavernous empty cinema. I sat alone, both feet dangling, mesmerised by a French dubbed version of *Moby Dick*. I tried to figure out what they were saying between the guttural grunts and nods. The lonely drama seemed to be played out just for me. An Odyssey within an odyssey, a dream within a dream. I was on my own as I often had been, but for the first time I didn't feel like an aimless lonely little soul searching for a half-forgotten dream. My own life at this point was no less thrilling than the film I was watching.

Luckily at seven I'd never heard of the *Titanic*, or I might have panicked when I saw my first huge iceberg. It looked as if someone had accidentally left a spare Frank Lloyd Wright construction lying around in the midst of those busy Atlantic sea lanes. I couldn't understand how nature had architected, then built this monstrous green triangular thing all by herself. The Ancients would probably have worshipped it on sight, whereas I just moved on to the next big thing, another cinema visit to watch a film, silent in all but music, entitled *The Red Balloon.*

At the time it embarrassed me, as it showed a side of childhood for what it really was, a series of dashed dreams often jealously punctured like the balloon itself, in this case by a gang of little thugs. Years later I came to realise I'd seen a positive masterpiece reflecting on how the protagonist, a thin rake of a boy, rises like a phoenix from the ashes in flight over the roof tops of Paris clutching a hundred coloured balloons or more.

Finally, our ship pulled slowly into port. A huge rainbow shower of confetti welcomed us weary travellers from the dock at Quebec. At first it looked like a huge slow-motion sports event, but then I realised the crowd had gathered to celebrate our arrival.

Crossing Canada to reach Vancouver took a further three days on the silver streamed Canadian Pacific Railway. The thing flew through cities, prairies, lakes, forests and mountain ranges. A large Perspex observation dome that brings to mind a 1950s idea of a spacecraft was available on the upper deck. Guess where I spent my three days? Yessiree!

Up there with the pines and the snow, I was travelling

through all the seasons in one journey. In the far distance the Rockies looked like up-turned Christmas puddings with lashings of cream on top. This wasn't just Disneyland's Rocky Mountain Railway ride, here was the real thing. No journey in later life could come close to the thrill of seeing the map of Canada unfold at my fingertips. My previous life in England felt artificially subterranean compared to this.

I took to Canada like a duck takes to water. The Wild West that I shared with all my newly made friends was in reality just a dirt track at the rear of all the clapboard wooden houses. I instantly became a Red Indian, surrounded by other young braves. We played with real air-rifles, and regularly took girls prisoner, only putting up a token resistance as we tied them up. In fact, nobody seemed to mind our savage, squealing antics.

Psychologically I'd burned my boats and wanted to forget all about the old country. I was enrolled in a very encouraging new school. I learned to sing "Oh Canada, Glorious and Free..." and believed every word of it. Over the four months we spent in Vancouver it was one long summer of beaches, Cheese-Wiz and fizzy drinks.

There was a local film house called the Hollywood Cinema. I thought I'd died, gone to heaven, then on to Hollywood. No-one told me the real Hollywood was in Los Angeles. Vancouver left me breathless. This was it — the land of the free. We'd seen the last of England... or had we?

Imagine my horror when suddenly Mum and Dad told me we were to return to England. I started having nightmares, fell out of bed imagining it was burning, like falling off a cliff into a grey world below. I had changed and I could never again be the introverted Pimlico boy who felt like the sum of his environment's confines within a treadmill in a concrete world no larger than that in the Truman Show movie.

The return crossing on the same ship had lost much of its glamour. The immaculate white uniforms of the crew now looked a little tarnished. The crossing was perpetually stormy. Sirens wailed, advising travellers to remain in their cabins. I ignored all warnings of course and privately skittled about on deck, whilst the boat was lashed by huge waves. Strangely the drama felt like watching just another film. In fact, I didn't particularly care if the waves were going to take me or not.

One night my harmonica fell off the table in the cabin and broke. The cracked casing on my Hohner Chromatic, the Rolls Royce of mouth organs, could no longer produce a pure tone. Simultaneously a deep fissure had broken into our cosy family life, never to be completely repaired. I missed Dad a lot already. He was to remain behind for a year paying off debts incurred with the Canadian government. There was a heavy price to pay for a family of returning immigrants.

Thousands emigrated, thousands returned. The simple fact is that Mum missed England, understandably as it was home, our roots. But all I could feel was motion sickness on the horrendous return voyage.

In London on the first day back at my old school, whilst climbing the stairs after assembly, I made the mistake of asking another inmate, "Where do we go?" I had not yet been assigned to a class. I was immediately arrested and hauled off to face a glowering white bristle haired devil of an art master called Huxtable. The sadistic old fucker then spanked me in front of his class with no explanation. Holding my tears in check, I thought, "Welcome back to England!" I'd been knocked right back to the beginning in this game of snakes and ladders some call destiny.

It was as if I was serving a prison sentence in a penal

colony from which I'd escaped. Once again enveloped by the London smog which was more noticeable on return, I felt strangely suffocated. It was like being thrown out of a temporary trip to Eden back into a murky Hell, where carefree enjoyment of life seemed like a distant dream. I no longer enjoyed childhood. I was tired of *Robin Hood* on Sunday TV, and even the clockwork train set had lost its shine. Cowboys and Indians had no place in that concrete world, flanked by the inevitability of school with the odd oasis of a weekend or holiday. Every day dragged on forever during the sentence of school... an oppressive Victorian building with high walls surrounding a tarmac playground.

I felt out of place at school. I was no good at ball games. To my father's disappointment I couldn't play football. He was good natured about it, but other kids gave me a hard time. I'd become a "geek". I wore glasses from age eight and kids at school called me "four eyes". Teachers were stern at best, at worst psychotic. I remember one of them, Mrs Denton, who assaulted us regularly and went to great pains to remind us that we were all losers. She looked just like Margaret Thatcher.

I escaped into films whenever I could. Father's mother took me to see several, including some of my favourites, *Forbidden Planet, Captain Clegg, Jason and the Argonauts*. I've used both *This Island Earth* and *Hercules Unchained* as titles of two of my tracks. I loved the science fiction and adventure fantasy stories, particularly the Greek myths and Sinbad adventures. Like my inner universe of dreams, the world of film gave some relief.

I was intrigued by *Superman* — the flying man of steel with the vulnerable heroine. I liked to imagine myself, throwing away my glasses and becoming the world's protector. I particularly liked *Batman* who had a darker aspect. I was interested in how he liked to hang around in caves and then would leap out of the darkness to the rescue. I liked to fantasise about owning a spaceship that would take me across the universe. I kept it in the back yard. Sometimes I'd invite a girl to join me on the flight. Having been led through a muddy puddle, past the garbage bins and around a corner she would gasp in amazement at my shiny vessel. I would lift her high above the dark, high buildings and take her beyond the sky above on to unexplored worlds. I was the hero of my dreams. I could rescue damsels in distress, break through walls and fly to the end of the universe.

But fantasies were only fleeting, whilst the world around me constantly crashed in. Not only was school a problem but family life was not the same after Canada, even after Dad returned home. At night I could hear my parents arguing. They had been apart for many months and their bond had been damaged. I found it difficult to sleep at night. Sometimes I felt paralysed by a force pressing down on my stomach in bed. It was as if some invisible monster was sitting on me. Dreams were disturbed with images of monsters or bodies on meat hooks left to die. I was fearful, but also angry. I couldn't find my centre. I sometimes stalked the streets aimlessly for hours. Disturbed with low self-esteem, I was susceptible to any bad influence that might come my way.

I befriended a maverick character. He was Artful Dodger to my Oliver Twist, so let's call him Dodger. Beyond the bombsites, bullies and beatings, another kind of darkness lurked beneath slippery river steps, through crevices between buildings and behind battered wooden doors. The world of Dickens wasn't just found in "all our yesterdays". It was still hovering close by, artfully dodging the taxman, eyeing potential victims passing by and waiting to sneak out at any given opportunity. When I wasn't playing mouth organ through the nose at school to win bets in the playground, I was quite studious, a good boy most of the time despite all my frustrations... until I met Dodger.

Dodger had eyes as wide as a fruit machine. We often disappeared off to the fairground to experience it in a new way. It was a bit like a *Lampwick* and *Pinocchio* situation, minus the donkey ears of course... Next to the Ghost Train was a little amusement arcade, where there was this kind of horse machine that may have been called the Winning Post. Hanging on the wall was something similar to a pinball machine that had horses. At one point the machine was broken. Dodger sussed that it would give you replays whether you deserved them or not. He was able to clap his hands and emulate the replay sound. He was a natural mimic. Even though he was just a kid he was always up to schemes and knew perfectly how to manipulate the world of adults. He was part entrepreneur, part pyromaniac! He once set fire to newspapers in the basement of a block of flats. He felt he could get away with a lot and he seemed to be pulling the strings of the adults. I don't think it was the other way around. My mother says he was almost like my first manager. He gave me an alternative education as arsonist, thief, Poker player and smoker, which for a nine-year-old was quite something!

So how did I get involved with him? It was a situation that crept up on me. When I first knew him, Dodger needed to be pushed around in a wheelchair due to something adults referred to in hushed tones as a bruised hip bone. As an initially reasonable sort I was elected at school to become his minder. I volunteered to push him in his chair and he then contrived to push me around in other ways. His parents gave into his every whim. His main aim was to exploit all his sympathetic supporters mercilessly. I think in a lot of ways he took his frustrations out on me.

Dodger's demands were endless, but he cleverly wielded power over me with his extensive record collection. My weakness was music and he knew it was my price. He already owned every new guitar record on the block. We listened to Duane Eddy's 'Because They're Young' (which eventually became the Luxembourg theme tune). This touched me deeply at the time. When I was listening to it I felt completely unmasked. It was the equivalent of being naked and realised I was red in the face. I couldn't look people in the eye as that exquisite melody came in. There's something about the orchestral part where it's joined by the rhythm. The beauty of it still makes my spine tingle when I think about it. The very title of the song got to me.

I loved everything by The Shadows and another favourite was 'Walk Don't Run' by the John Barry Seven way before Barry hit the Big Time with the *James Bond* films. That guitar really worked for me. The lead guitarist was Vic Flick. It was that little moment from the tremolo arm that really got me. Dodger often became furious when my tastes didn't coincide with his, but he was on safe ground with any record that featured electric guitars. So much the better if it was electric guitar with orchestra which to this day remains a lifelong influence.

Music with Dodger was also an important part of the funfair. The variety of musical sounds coming from different directions, all of it like a huge collage of sound, which was so aptly described on The Beatles 'Being for the Benefit of Mr. Kite!'.

This thing about the power of music comes in here. The more one went to the funfair the more one was aware of the music that was being played. The first Stones album was a big favourite there, along with Martha and the Vandellas' 'Dancing In The Street'.

My friends and I were all too young to have relationships with girls, but those songs seemed to egg you on. "Every guy grab a girl…" The chorus was so compelling, and what a beautiful song! I've noticed it's one of Mike Rutherford's favourites as well. I think it speaks to him in the same way as it does me. The arrangement is perfect. It's Tamla Motown at its best. The fairground had the rides, but the songs were our invisible fuel.

One summer via one of Dodger's connections I briefly got to work beside the fairground in the amusement arcade. Here we often heard songs like 'Pipeline' by The Shantays and 'Wipeout' by The Safaris, with its manic laugh at the beginning. In its simplicity it wombled along, but it didn't seem to matter. It was a dumb kind of melody that everyone could cotton on to, a bit like Chris Montez singing 'Let's Dance', with the most banal organ riff in the world, one that was parodied much later by Bruce Springsteen with 'Glory Days'.

The arcade job was one of my first, and between the moments when I had to dish out change, I strode about the area in a khaki coat, proud that I'd become a part of the fairground's inner sanctum. The guy who owned the arcade showed me what to do when someone lost their penny in one of these little machines where there was something you'd flick, and you'd be rewarded by a stale half broken cigarette. As part of my audition my boss said, "Do you know how to keep your eyes and ears open and your mouth shut?" I said 'yes' and indeed, taking my job seriously, I hardly ever engaged anyone in conversation. I noticed that he regularly disappeared off to the back of the wooden shack-like arcade building with a particularly well-endowed lady friend…

Dodger and I might have shared a love of music and the funfair, but ultimately, we were different animals. Dodger's total lack of conscience worried me. On one occasion, when he was sneering and swearing at an old lady on crutches who'd been upset by his taunts, I knew that I should pull away from him. I apologised to the woman on his behalf.

My eyes were opening at that time to the plight of several lonely elderly people living in that alienated concrete jungle. Maybe that's partly why The Beatles' song 'Eleanor Rigby' has always touched me so much. Another pal of mine, Brian Dunn, had an aunt who lived on her own in a tiny room under the stairs with no windows. She had nothing for company except a small oil fire heater. She was too frightened to step outside in case the bombs might still fall. We couldn't convince her otherwise.

Not only was isolation and poverty still a big problem despite the achievements of the late forties, but other things were slow to change too. People still thought smoking was good for you, radiation was regarded as so safe that feet were x-rayed in shoe shops, and the death penalty was the norm for murder.

I was still just nine years of age when I read in a paper about a guy, Podola, who was about to be hanged. The mere thought of executions appalled me and I felt sorry for him. He was trying to commit suicide in advance of his execution. People would say to me that this was a natural consequence of a capital crime, but I always felt that two wrongs never made a right, plus many innocent people such as Timothy Evans were brutally executed. I was relieved when that barbaric practice ended in the UK.

London was still polluted and fog ridden. Chimney stacks continued to belch out fumes. When I was around

31

the age of ten, we moved into a place beside Ebury Bridge overlooking the railway near Victoria Station, which was regularly engulfed by steam from the trains. They shunted and grunted below, and an alarm bell went off in the middle of the night. Visitors wondered how we slept at all! Bridge House was to be my home for the rest of my childhood, throughout my teens and into my early twenties.

You'd think I had very little chance of making it out of that environment, but if I had a motto it would have read, "*Never* let other people's limitations become your own". To borrow a leaf from Peter Cook and Dudley Moore, or rather their alter egos Derek and Clive, it may be partly because I come from that strange mongrel world, a mixed background where Lord Snooty and pals rubbed shoulders in the streets with Dennis the Menace, whilst the Krays still ruled the West End. Opposite ends of the social spectrum lived side by side in Pimlico. Post war London held a regular jumble sale of classes and crazed characters. Just up the road from Bridge House was Buckingham Palace. Diplomats and celebrities alike lived just a stone's throw away from council tenants.

I was aware of all the possibilities life held. Determined not to be pulled down by boys like Dodger, who was destined to deal drugs at the local secondary school, I worked hard to get through my Eleven Plus and I was glad to get a place at Sloane Grammar School. I hoped that place would give me a better chance…

3

A sea of dreams...

Starting at the grammar school felt like a new world of possibilities ahead, but there were still plenty of challenges. The good came with the bad. The school seemed fine at first with a kindly headmaster with walrus moustache who loved music and theatre. But soon after I arrived, he retired. A very different kind of character took his place.

New headmaster Doc Henry represented everything I wanted to rebel against. Although he'd been a Japanese prisoner of war, he was a dead ringer for Heinrich Himmler. He even wore the same wire framed glasses. All that was missing was the leather great coat. We referred to him as Herr Doktor. He was universally disliked by pupils and masters alike. MP and fellow inmate at Sloane Alan Johnson remembers him as The Dreaded in his autobiography. His reign of terror was similar to Count Dracula's. We'd be enjoying ourselves in the playground, birds tweeting nearby... Suddenly a deathly silence would descend, the temperature plummeting along with the birds as his dark shadow loomed. Creeping up behind unsuspecting groups of small boys, breathing fire down their collars, he spat venom from a great height. They staggered backwards. Beatings and executions were to follow for minor infringements of unwritten rules... Lunchtime was for drinking and caning. Teaching was a mere secondary pastime for him. He taught both Latin and French. Later on, the thought of two years of French with him at the helm was to put me off following through A Levels.

Thankfully, not all schoolmasters were like Doc Henry. One day when I was bored out of my skull on the football field, one of the lads asked the teacher, "if you could choose your favourite way to die, what would it be?" Quick as a flash with a deadpan expression he answered, "To be shot in the back at the point of orgasm in intercourse..."

The antithesis to Doc Henry was one of the most extraordinary guys I've ever known. Péter Pallai, my history teacher, a survivor of the Holocaust and fugitive from the 1956 Hungarian uprising, was an inspiration to us all. A keen sportsman who'd honed his canooing skills up to Olympic standard, he was a strong charismatic character with an aversion to lazy boys, and a passion for his subject.

He stood out in my memory for a long time after my school days. Then by an amazing coincidence we reconnected many years down the line due to a musical connection. He'd left teaching to become a jazz presenter for the BBC World Service. I'm proud to say we're still friends to this day and we often touch base in both London and Budapest.

Another encouraging teacher was young Johnny Bolland my gym master. As previously mentioned, I was useless at football and cricket (much to Dad's disappointment) but after a ton of hard work I became a member of the school gymnastics team. I wanted to be able to fly like Nureyev. I kept pushing myself to perform ever more difficult manoeuvres and on a good day could do a complete somersault in the air. These days my gymnastics have moved on to the fingers and I still aim to jump through impossible hoops. I guess the whole thing of pushing the boundaries has always been a big thing for me.

A mountaineering friend Andrew nearly reached the top of Everest, but he chose to rescue a fellow climber who would otherwise have perished. Soon after, Andrew returned to complete his task and reached the peak. I admire his spirit. Much in life I find is about pitting yourself against the elements, meeting unexpected challenges, scaling the peaks and forging ahead into unchartered territory.

During my early time at Sloane Grammar I didn't know what to do with my restless spirit. Beyond the gymnastics I vented frustration through mixing with 'School Bully' and his band of merry henchmen who liked to do nothing better than have a regular playground punch-up. Pretty early on I realised this was getting me nowhere and I didn't like the way they treated other kids. This wasn't my way, but I had an enormous amount of pent up energy that was bursting to be released.

My angst found different outlets. From the age of twelve onwards I lapped up all the horror films at the Biograph in Victoria, London's oldest cinema built in 1905. I was obviously below the age of eighteen but they let me in without challenge, as with local pubs. There was a less stringent policy on keeping out youngsters in those days.

The horror movies weren't a cure but gave a safe focus for my frustrations. The first horror movie I saw was a Hammer production *Curse of the Werewolf* which I believe was Oliver Reed's first starring role. Gothic and obviously unreal, it was like an extension of fairy tales with death as symbol rather than reality. I can see how still today teenagers get attracted to the Gothic genre. They have demons to face and rejection in love, flying the coop, going it alone and finding they have to deal with all the problems the world throws at us all.

I saw monsters of the Id in Doc Henry and every teacher who'd given me a hard time. I felt oppressed by darkest Pimlico and there was the underlying terror that I might never get out. I saw others around me start to turn to drugs. I never wanted to go down that road, but it was as if some unnamed shadow was frantically knocking on my door. Since childhood I'd been attacked by waking nightmares of sound waves, relentlessly coming for me. There was something missing, a silent voice within begging me to listen. By my early teens something inside me was screaming to find expression.

At this time I bought my first guitar, and miraculously the nightmares began to subside.

Initially, my Dad kindly gave me an acoustic guitar he had brought back from Canada, but the action on it was absolutely brutal with really heavy strings. Dad said if I practised enough, I'd get callouses on my fingers but six months later they remained just open wounds. But I was still undeterred.

I was relieved to acquire one which had an easier action. It was a Japanese semi acoustic. The shop assistant broke the news that I would need an amp. It had never occurred to me. Ever practical, I'd assumed you just plugged into the wall and it would magically make the right noise! Your friends would be amazed. When I first plugged it in the amp started to howl with a high whistling sound... The shop guy informed me this was called feedback. There were a few things to learn.

I started to really go for guitar from age fourteen onwards. It was a liberating feeling. I'd opened the door to a whole new world and adolescent horrors transformed into creative fervour. Both parents were a great support, a big boost to confidence and ambition. Whilst Dad helped to instigate the playing, Mum regularly suggested I perform to family and friends. Later, once John was up and running on guitar and flute as well, she thoroughly encouraged the two of us.

I came to the guitar through a love of the electric instrument and the fab players of the time. The first time I heard a guitar solo that really sounded perfect was Brian Jones on 'I Wanna Be Your Man'. It screamed like a Harley Davidson... The Stones were lucky to have two guitarists who were equally adept at blowing me away. My favourite Keith Richards' solo was on 'Route 66'. The Stones with their rebellious vibe and electric guitars blazing, became a symbol of freedom for me.

One defining moment came when I was practising Keith's 'Route 66' guitar licks at school with my pal Paul Swinson. We were playing in the music room after hours. We'd been allowed to hook up our guitars to the record player and the Tannoy system. As I was blasting way in the middle of Keith's solo thinking 'this is good, I'm really cracking it now', I saw Paul's face fall. I realised something had gone terribly wrong and turned to see the headmaster who was purple with rage. He thundered towards us, shrieking, "I was four floors up, trying to talk to the staff, couldn't hear myself think with that racket going on! What do the two of you think you're doing?" The response was all mumbled apologies with our heads hung low. However, it was at that moment I realised that as this was the very thing that displeased Doc Henry so much, it had to be worth becoming a future career.

A new world was opening up. Each night when I returned from school the *real* work would start. Every time

I walked out of the school gates, I couldn't wait to get home and pick up the guitar. It was something I was never going to be graded in. No one was ever going to slap my wrist or give me a C minus or an F or an A for it. I was either going to enjoy it or I wasn't going to do it. My drive was now focussed through a total fascination with the sounds I aimed to get out of the beast. I so much wanted to emulate Hank Marvin and Brian Jones, and to unlock all their secrets... I'd practise for hours, not noticing the time passing by. Cups of tea Mum brought in would go cold.

Moved as I was by blues and rock, classical music also affected me deeply from an early age. When I was very small, I loved hearing Kathleen Ferrier singing as well as Mario Lanza. Later, when I was about eight years old living on the Tatchbrook estate, there was a boy we didn't see much of. He seemed to be happier to stay at home as he was in a wheelchair after suffering from Polio. He once said he had a piece of music he wanted me to listen to. We went into his dark, dingy room. I remember him showing me his legs, which were matchstick thin. That was a bit disconcerting, but the next minute he put a piece of music on a wind-up gramophone, which was every bit as good and even better than he had described it. It was Tchaikovsky's *Piano Concerto in B Flat Minor*. There was something about the way the orchestra came soaring in with that fantastic melody.

Suddenly it felt that there was no difference between him and me. It wasn't as if I could walk and he couldn't. At that moment, of course, we both flew with the angels. From that time on, I've always loved Tchaikovsky's music. It was healing and uplifting. There was something melancholic about it, but also passionate and triumphant.

I was led to classical music by degrees.

The next big event in terms of classical music was in 1965, when I was listening to the pop music of the day and was learning the Keith Richards licks. At this time my mother's friend Joy lent me the album, *Segovia plays Bach*. Straight away from the first melody it made me aware that the guitar was seemingly as versatile as the keyboard in terms of the things it could cover. It didn't sound just like a guitar in Segovia's hands. It sounded almost like a keyboard, but sweeter. It was heartfelt and seemed as if all of nature was speaking through his instrument with a kind of refined innocence.

I marvelled then and still do at the different tones he was able to conjure from the instrument. His technique seemed to circumvent the problems that the guitarist has, accessing independent bass lines and top lines. This stuff had been recorded in the 1920s and 1930s when he was at the peak of his technique.

When I was listening to Segovia's version of Bach pieces that had originally been largely written for violin and cello, I decided that I could either spend the rest of my life trying to do what he had already done perfectly so many years earlier, or else I could take that influence forward.

I was to come up with original pieces that were highly influenced by his efforts, such as my album *Tribute*. On it I recorded Bach pieces including the most difficult and extraordinary of them all, 'The Chaconne'. Once I'd started recording it, I learned that the piece was written to commemorate the death of his wife. That may give some clues as to why the piece starts off doomily and then becomes unbearably sweet. It needs a very moving approach to playing.

My discovery of tapping was initially through playing something Bach-like. I realised that you could make each string travel further by hammering on and off with both hands on the fretboard, either with the nail or the pad of the finger. Mastering that, I realised I could do this on both acoustic and electric guitar, each totally different to the other, but styles cross over, and I became equally addicted to playing both electric and classical... Bring on the drug! There's no cure!

At times it's kept me up all night, and other times it's woken me up like a gentle six stringed sister. Progressive, Bach, Blues or beyond... That's the endless story... reconfiguring memories Bach to the future...

Of course, music wasn't the only thing in my life. Teenage life was kicking in. My early idea of going out for a drink with my mates sometimes had disastrous results. On one occasion a pal and I worked our way through a crate load of Scotch and Asti Spumante. I didn't have any idea of the strength of the stuff and my head immediately started to spin as I headed off for home. Lurching along the street, barely able to walk, I spied two girls I knew. I immediately threw my arms around them both, and they virtually carried me back home. I don't think I was a good proposition for either of them!

I was keen to find a girlfriend from an early age. Although Sloane Grammar was a 'boys only' school, my first year there did offer a close proximity to girls and an early awareness of them, as Carlisle School for girls backed on to our school divided by a Berlin wall.

My earliest forays into exploring the mystery of woman had started when I was about three years old and an aunt visited our flat with a new boyfriend. I decided to break the ice, hovering around her knees. Like lightning I reached up her skirt and felt something hard at the top of her stocking. Having no idea that I'd found the clasp at the

40

end of her suspender belt I asked in all innocence, "Is that your winkie?" My poor aunt turned scarlet. Borrowing from the toddler's handbook of how to make the party go with a swing I'd managed to ruin the evening.

I always liked to converse with girls. You played games with boys but you talked to girls. They seemed to be way ahead. As a glasses wearer from the age of eight I felt like an outsider. There were taunts like "Four eyes!" and "Hackett, penny a packet!" Boys are bastards!

Connecting with girls as a male was even harder. I was shy. I wasn't sure at first what I was supposed to find attractive or how to relate. I snatched the odd kiss, but I didn't know what to do next. When I did start to be genuinely interested, I desperately wanted a partner, but I'd fall apart with embarrassment whenever I came close. Finally, I got myself together and mustered up the courage...

My first girlfriend Barbara lived near my home. It was one of those strange double-edged days when I finally plucked up the courage to ask her out. I had a Saturday job at the time in a local shop. Being my usual impractical self, having crushed a box of eggs beneath a pile of heavy shopping in a customer's bag, I was sacked... But Barbara smiled and said, "Yes!" So, on the day I lost the job, I didn't care because I had the girl...

When I first met her at age fifteen, she looked and sounded very posh and attended Putney High School for Girls. She'd won a scholarship to the school, was already widely read and admirably bright. I was impressed by her intelligence. I had great hopes for her, and she pointed the way. She challenged me to read books by writers like Jean Paul Sartre and Camus, encouraging me to broaden my mind. From the time I was involved with Barbara onwards I maintained a life-long interest in reading books and visiting art galleries. She lived in an apartment block called Jane Austen House, an appropriate name for her home and an inspiration for the title of the song 'Jane Austen's Door'.

We shared the love of music too. The two of us used to get drunk on gin and orange in a haze of tobacco smoke listening endlessly to The Rolling Stones, The Beatles, The Byrds, Buffy Sainte-Marie, Bach and Segovia for hours at my parents' place. She was learning cello at school. In fact, I thought she looked like Jacqueline du Pré. She sat for hours watching as I played guitar in front of her — probably eventually boring her to death! But she held me captive as much as the instrument I played…

Shared creativity, intellect and ideas worked well, but she was way ahead of me in the personal sense. I was a naive virgin and she led the way. She was far less inhibited than me. At age sixteen I lost my virginity to her. I was so absorbed with the relationship that I couldn't concentrate on my 'O' level exams, just about managing to get English Lit, English Lang, French and Spanish. My history teacher who had until now been pleased with my progress, looked at me with an expression of despondency and asked, "Are you in love Hackett?" in front of the whole class. I blushed.

Unfortunately, my reverie was short lived. That summer I lost Barbara to an older guy, who had a car, his own place and an impressive Blues album collection. I felt a bit like Tom in the *Tom and Jerry* cartoon when he's saved up like crazy to by an old banger to impress the white cat, but he's swept aside and crushed by a super cool cat in shiny ultra-long stretch limo! I didn't even have a banger, I lived in my parents' flat where John and I shared a bedroom, and I was still spotty as hell.

Pete was Barbara's way out. She left home to move in with him, and there she fully embraced her rebellion against her posh polo-playing family background in a haze of drink, drugs and smoke. I was gutted. I sat alone listening to Buffy Sainte-Marie singing "Must I go bound and you go free..." night after night. We continued a communication, but it prolonged my agony because I kept hoping she would come back to me. She kept me dangling, occasionally suggesting that we might get back together at some point.

Finally, I reached a turning point. A couple of years had passed by and I visited Barbara when she was in hospital undergoing a drug cure. It had taken me ages to get there by public transport (yes, still no banger). She was talking to a counsellor. I said hello and with an expression of irritation she complained that my appearance was an interruption which ruined the great conversation she was having. I immediately left. It was one of those defining moments in life when you cross a threshold and there's no looking back. I decided there and then that next time she wouldn't hear from me, she would hear *about* me.

Indeed, I didn't see her again until I was in Genesis at the Lincoln Festival in 1972. She turned up, and subsequently wrote to me saying "Your fame is blown out all over the high streets!" She was now as impressed as she'd once been dismissive. It was my Heathcliff moment. I didn't want to get even, but I no longer felt humiliated by her and I wasn't pining for her anymore. At last she couldn't hurt me.

The irony of my teen relationship situation is that each girlfriend had a link to the same guy who took Barbara from me. In the case of one girl, Sue, I started to date her only to discover that he had already made her pregnant! Then he and another girlfriend of his decided to set me up on a blind date. I was so embarrassed by the idea that I turned up with a bunch of friends. Despite this unpromising beginning, my blind date Juliette and I did strike up a relationship. We stayed together for a while, although her mind was often on other things. It was a bit like going out with Ruby Tuesday. She never said where she came from and I didn't know her surname. She loved the film *Far From The Madding Crowd* and dreamed of Alan Bates and Terence Stamp. Memories of girls like Barbara and Juliette fed my idea for the song 'Fantasy' on my album *Beyond the Shrouded Horizon*... all those girls who can never quite realise the fantasies they seek.

I know we all have fantasies and dreams. Some of them run through our fingers like water, as in my dream of a perfect world with Barbara. Others flower and blossom into life's exciting adventure, with all its challenges and rewards.

My dream of a musical path was already an obsession by the time I left school.

One place Barbara introduced me to which left a lasting musical impression on me was a venue in an old hotel on Eel Pie Island in Twickenham. I remember talking to one of the older residents of the island from the days when dance bands used to play there, and he said, "It all got ruined when Mick Jagger and his mob moved in."

Indeed, the venue did go through several changes, from the swing era, which in its turn was to give way to rhythm and blues. I loved its sinister quality. I feel that the House Of Blues places in the States have retained the spooky voodoo atmosphere that Eel Pie once had.

From about sixteen I enjoyed the concerts on Eel Pie about once every two weeks on a Sunday. There was always the concern that I might not be able to get in, but I looked a bit old for my age, so I passed for eighteen. I guess they were also trying to pack as many people in as they could, so chose not to look too closely!

The first time I ventured forth to that place was like

an initiation. I could hear this wonderful blues music playing in the distance through the cold and the mist from the other side of the Thames. Crossing the footbridge to Eel Pie, one reached a point at the end where there was a charcoal brazier, beside which sat an old woman. She held out her hand and asked for 'a penny, dear'. She cannot have made much doing that, but it felt like a rite of passage, similar to the Greek myth of those paying the ferryman a coin to take them across the River Styx to the land of the dead.

That island was a world of its own. As I paid the penny toll and began to walk forward along a dimly lit path, the music grew louder. I'd hear the strains of a guitar playing a slow blues. It sounded incredibly enticing. Even though I've played notes like that all my life, the setting of the place on this island where it all happened still haunts me. Years later, with my track 'Fire Island' on *To Watch the Storms*, I renamed Eel Pie 'Fire Island', because the music for sure set me on fire.

Entering the inner sanctum where the band was playing, it was like going into a witch's coven. The magic was there in the music, and in contrast to the cold outside the place was warm and full of life. There were also strange, primitive things on the wall that were less like décor and more like graffiti, but there seemed to be a strange, sinister quality to the designs. I can easily imagine why John Mayall ended up writing things like 'I'm Your Witch Doctor', or how Peter Green would later come up with 'Black Magic Woman'.

The place was a ramshackle dive with sawdust on the floor and the smell of disinfectant where they'd hand you a drink like Newcastle Brown Ale in a bottle with no glass. There were no seats, so in many ways it was an uncomfortable place. You stood there listening to the music, getting increasingly drunk. However, the really intoxicating thing was not just the beer and the sound of the Blues, but something else beyond that. It was a perfect low-key setting for people such as Eric Clapton and Peter Green to cut their teeth.

I saw the amazing Paul Butterfield Blues Band at Eel Pie, playing to a handful of people. Apparently, Butterfield had the first mixed race band in Chicago. I showed up quite early and I saw a guy leaning up against a pillar and looking rather uncomfortable and out of place there. He had that clean-cut American college boy look. I was later to learn that was the late great Mike Bloomfield. In those days, being a sixteen-year-old, I was too embarrassed to approach and engage anyone in conversation. I wish I had now!

In those days, people didn't do sound checks. A band would amble on and play a couple of licks; then they would start up. That was a cursory kind of ritual. However, when Butterfield and his band came on it seemed like they took ages to set up. Bloomfield and the other guitarist Elvin Bishop were both firing off powerful blues licks, just on their own.

Initially Butterfield didn't play one note on the harmonica. But when he got going, it was like being flattened by a truck. Butterfield's harmonica was extraordinary. I'd been playing harmonica virtually all my life, but this guy was re-inventing the instrument in front of me. The exceptional tone was loud, raucous and sounded more like a cross between a trumpet and a guitar. He had such an amazing range with incredible vibrato.

Most of the time audiences were too cool to show much appreciation. But, on that night at Eel Pie everyone ran to the front of the stage to watch what was going on. An American friend of mine described the experience of watching Butterfield playing as a master flanked by two guitarists trying to steal the limelight like baying dogs. In those days, guitarists generally stood still as they played, but these guys were bopping around! It was one of those terrifically intense experiences. I'd never seen anything like it before... and haven't since. It was as if those guys were completely possessed. They played like nothing on earth. Whenever I play Blues even now, I'm always trying to get back to that night. Now Paul and Mike have gone with whatever it was that shortened their lives. It's too easy to write people off with comments like "Yeah, Bloomfield was a speed freak" and "Butterfield's weakness was drink". Butterfield's work is legendary, and Bob Dylan who he collaborated with said that Bloomfield was his favourite guitarist.

Peter Green playing with John Mayall's Blues Breakers at Eel Pie also had me transfixed. I started going to gigs around the time that Green had taken over from Clapton in that band. Clapton was a hard act to follow, but watching Peter Green play his Les Paul was equally inspiring. He seemed to be doing everything I wanted to be able to do, but I had neither the experience nor the equipment.

Green seemed to be doing some strange things like waggling his hand as he was sustaining a note. At that time, I had no idea what that was. Eventually it dawned on me that he was vibrating the string, pulling it up and down. One thing I practise more than anything else especially when recording, is finger vibrato, particularly when bending a string up a tone whilst trying to get that truly magical sound that's so elusive at first.

As for Eric Clapton, he created a searing sound live, again with Les Paul guitar and Marshall amp. You hear this to great effect on the John Mayall album where Eric is reading the *Beano* on the front. Those who love it know it as "the Beano album"! It has fantastic fiery blues playing on it. To my mind Eric is at his best on that.

It would be impossible not to mention Jeff Beck. I first heard his stuff live with The Yardbirds on *Ready, Steady, Go*. I was a little bit too young to go to gigs, but the *Roger the Engineer* album they made had some wonderful solos by Jeff. There was great use of distortion, feedback, reverb and repeat echoes. It seemed that there was occasionally a fuzz box tone, transformed when reverb and repeat echo were added. It ended up sounding almost like an Indian instrument. He has an outstanding solo on 'Shapes of Things', where some notes sound chillingly like a woman's voice.

What I now hear as pure feedback, my young mind had transformed into this magical, eerie, ghostly sound that has inspired and influenced me. Jeff hit some incredible notes and his tone was ground-breaking. He's always managed to do something extraordinary with that mechanical beast the electric guitar, particularly with the whammy bar. He still makes the guitar squeal and jump, thrilling several generations of guitarists.

During my mid to late teens I rehearsed in the evenings like crazy, trying to get a band together that had enough cover versions of songs for gigs. There was a fair smattering of Paul Butterfield tunes, songs by The Byrds or The Moody Blues, and even the odd original piece, written by guys who passed through the band or by myself. It was a formative time before I turned twenty. A new universe was constantly unfolding. Music seemed every bit as magical as toys had once been.

At first, I tended to favour the more Blues-based acts because that was where guitar was at its most cutting edge. But by 1966 the world was moving into a new era and music

48

was changing... Totally new sounds were emerging. The Beatles album *Revolver* marked a distinct musical turning point. I was fascinated by all the new sounds emerging.

Sergeant Pepper was a defining piece of work. I loved songs like 'Being For The Benefit Of Mr Kite' and 'She's Leaving Home', which are strongly visual and tell stories. The narrative reigns supreme on those tunes. It colours my approach these days in song to romance of places. The Beatles had already harnessed the use of orchestral instruments and planted the seeds of world music.

The first time I heard *Sergeant Pepper*, which proved to be a hugely influential album and really defined the sixties in terms of the sound, was at the Chelsea Antiques Market. I walked upstairs to one of the rooms, full of suspended Indian silks. A strange sounding piece of music was wafting through the atmosphere as I was surrounded by exotic incense and colour. It turned out to be 'Within You Without You' from *Sergeant Pepper.* It was a perfect combination of the time, the setting, the clothes and the music, which defined that era that seemed to paint a rainbow on every corner.

King's Road was the hub of the changing times. Travelling up that road every day I saw the sixties taking shape. I noticed a growing number of boutiques, restaurants and cafés springing up. Clothes were becoming ever more colourful, shocking and surprising (unlike today's uniformity).

Once I'd done my homework in a cursory manner, I liked to wander off along King's Road at night, with the intriguingly unusual things for sale in the windows. I didn't want to own any of it, but this impossibly exotic world was so close, on the other side of the tracks, just around the corner. It was as if with a few steps, as in C.S. Lewis' *The Lion, the Witch and the Wardrobe*, I'd walked through a wardrobe into another universe.

As now, there was the Royal Court Theatre on Sloane Square, with its fountain. I still think it is one of the prettiest of London's squares. To one side of the Royal Court Theatre, you walked by the Holbein Cellars shop with its beautiful Dickensian facade. I was still a young school kid when I looked at this place, thinking how good it would be one day to walk in there and sample some of their finest wines! Wandering past the Pizza Express in Fulham Road, which was the first in London, my face was pressed against the window. Pizza seemed so exotic at that time.

On one occasion when I was walking along Kings Road I saw Brian Jones, looking very dapper in a black suit. I passed Mick Jagger by the *Peter Jones* department store, resplendent in double breasted blazer and shades. He was every inch the rock star, whilst I was still in my less than thrilling grey school uniform thinking, 'this won't do! I've got to get out of these togs as quickly as possible, I must leave school and get myself into a band.'

I'd already fallen in love with the Stones' music without knowing what they looked like. I'd bought 'Not Fade Away', but I was more interested in the B side, 'Little by Little'. The sound of the harmonica thrilled me on it — like hearing a clarion call from the underworld.

Seeing them live on TV on *Ready Steady Go* was another kind of experience. I saw strength in their faces individually that other acts didn't have. Like The Beatles, they had an extra level of energy. A lot of bands just stood there looking wooden and grateful to be there. The Stones also had a compelling, confrontational aura about them. Far from being intimidated, they obviously loved the camera, and the camera loved them back. Both seeing the Stones on TV and passing them in Kings Road were defining moments.

I was convinced I wanted to be a guitarist in a world class band...

One place I remember from that time in Kings Road was Guys and Dolls, a small sandwich bar, but it was there that I heard some great tracks on the radio for the first time. One was Cream's 'Strange Brew'.

My friend Gordon and I were sitting in Guys and Dolls one day when we heard a Jeff Beck solo from 'Tallyman', and we wondered if he was using a slide. This was early harmony guitar work that must have also influenced Brian May, who I worked with much later.

I remember the Mary Quant shop on the corner of Markham Square, where apparently, she worked all night to produce goods to sell the next day. In the Sixties it seemed that a lot of people sprang from obscurity on to front page headlines. Many like Mary Quant and Vidal Sassoon, all worked their socks off to achieve the position they held.

About a year or so later between the years 1967 and 1968, when Flower Power was at its height, I'd walk down Kings Road, often passing incense filled doorways and hearing the sound of jingling as people wandered by with their kaftans and bells. I think it took a lot of guts to fully embrace the look at that time because British opinion was polarised. The working man in the street was offended by this new look. Sometimes someone would pick a fight with me just because I had long hair. This happened especially when guys had had a little too much to drink. It was a very tricky time. Things were changing. The old guard was still very much in evidence. It wasn't until about 1969 that I was able to hold down a job and allowed to wear my hair as long as I wanted.

At this time I enjoyed experimenting with pretty questionable clothes choices, such as a pair of orange flairs that were so tight, I couldn't sit down in them. I was keen to buy a leather jacket and a sweet young guy with a distinctive face I always remembered sold me one at Kensington Market. Later on, I realised that this was none other than Freddie Mercury!

I met him again years on when I was recording with GTR, and Queen, who were also recording at the Townhouse, came to my birthday party. Thinking of Freddie singing "Who wants to live forever..." I find a poignant reminder of someone who should have lived so much longer. But back in the late 1960s everything felt possible and an endless future lay ahead for us all.

In those times it was all about drinking, parties, trying on people like clothes... The Rolling Stones and The Beatles were in a way like Pied Pipers leading the dance.

In the mid to late Sixties whilst the arts and particularly music were exploding with creative ideas, in parallel Vietnam was exploding with bombs each day. America's surrogate war seemed inevitable given the way political thinking was so polarised. "Better dead than red" was the US policy at the time. Paranoid politics ruled the day.

Along with several friends I joined an anti-war rally. As part of the surging throng we trooped through London's Hyde Park towards Grosvenor Square. Clashes with police were inevitable and I remember many people were hurt. The important thing was that London was registering its own protest against an unnecessary war which claimed too many lives on both sides. Many years later I was to organise *Rock Against Repatriation* to help Vietnamese "Boat People" in their attempted flight to freedom and their heavy-handed treatment by Hong Kong authorities whilst Britain still held sway in the region. Depleted Vietnam deserved a better deal from the West than the hand it had been dealt so far.

The sixties was an extraordinary time musically. Music was growing up. We were no longer being subjected to a diet of exclusively mating oriented material. Serious concerns were now a strong part of the picture. Peace songs like Dylan's 'Blowin' In The Wind' were both poetically and politically powerful. Buffy Sainte-Marie's protest songs such as 'Now That The Buffalo's Gone' helped to bring social concerns to the fore. Love songs were now standing side by side with songs concerning humanity as a whole.

King Crimson's 'Epitaph' was incredibly powerful with its bleak message of mankind's doomed future. Lyricist Pete Sinfield surpassed himself with that track. "The fate of all mankind I see is in the hands of fools..." Once again today the rise of extremists poses a real threat to world peace. Conflicting ideologies abound in a polarised world of haves and have nots. Invade a country, destroy its infrastructure, bomb the hell out of it, lock up thousands of people in camps... breeding grounds for evil acts of terrorism. You never know what you might inadvertently unleash...

Surely, history teaches that nothing exists in isolation. There is always an unseen consequence. Resentment festers. Martyrs abound. Dylan's 'With God On Our Side' sneers at the self-righteous. Beware the lethal combination of God and guns. Politicians can justify anything. We need writers with songs of a comparable stature or else 'Epitaph', with its grim world view might still become a reality. Vietnam is not the West's only mistake. Remember the joke about the world's first national anthem? "God bless all those in cave 13 and to hell with all the rest!" There are no longer refugees. The press now calls them 'migrants' or worse 'economic migrants'. We need more compassion, not less. A fortress mentality can only lead to more bloodshed.

I feel the world's future lies in the balance more so now than ever before. My recent songs 'Behind The Smoke', 'West To East' and 'Beasts In Our Time' address global issues. And it's not just me. Songs can change the world. Peter Gabriel's 'Biko' for instance, sombre yet visionary. Pink Floyd's 'On the Turning Away'… Both home grown but both with a message beyond mere entertainment.

But back in 1969 I didn't feel particularly empowered. It was just two years before I finally turned into a professional muso. I was working as a chain man for a City Hall surveyor. At least it got me out into the open air instead of feeling incarcerated in an office dreaming of a future in music. I was banging yet another nail into the tarmac whilst trying not to smash my fingers when a pal spotted me.

"Hello Steve, why are you wasting your time doing that? Come and see a band called King Crimson at the Marquee on Sunday and I promise you won't be disappointed!" I took his advice and he turned out to be right of course.

Crimson were different to the usual blues-based bands I'd admired so far. The music was eclectic, disciplined and poetic, yet anarchic in places. They had a pan-genre approach that allowed them to draw from Jazz, Rock and Classical with a hint of Beatles plus a touch of dance hall at the end of the pier. Very British but with an outsider's edge.

That first evening was also my first encounter with the all-important Mellotron which was to play a large part in my development. An orchestra in a box with a steely cold yet powerful distillation of symphonic possibilities. It was an incredible night. At one point in the show, someone handed Greg Lake a piece of paper. To my recollection, he then said, "The Americans have just landed on the moon. I'm sure we all wish them the best of luck." The band then began playing 'Epitaph'. In one momentary flash, I could feel how humanity was capable of the most extraordinary things, from reaching the heights of sublime achievements to plummeting into the depths of potential cataclysm.

There were extraordinary free concerts in Hyde Park seemingly every other week. I saw Jethro Tull, Pink Floyd, Blind Faith, Traffic, The Nice and eventually the Stones, sadly shortly after Brian Jones had tragically passed on. I loved his slide guitar work, his multi-instrumental talent and his sense of style. A big star had gone out in the night sky, starting an alarming trend that the counter-culture couldn't reverse. Falling stars would soon be all around. For Baby Boomers the roll call of the rock 'n roll dead started in '69 with Brian's untimely departure. Brian was arguably murdered, but he was certainly a self-poisoner.

Whilst I just missed Brian, I got to see Jimi Hendrix only a few weeks before his untimely death in 1970. If the Americans had Woodstock in '69, we had the Isle of Wight festival in '70, with Jimi Hendrix headlining. It had to be visited with its dazzling array of mainly British acts, including Jethro Tull, The Who, Free, Moody Blues, plus American Richie Havens who had opened Woodstock the previous year and who later became a great friend.

It was Jimi Hendrix's last big gig. In a matter of weeks, the master of the Blues would pass, far too early for the young trailblazer he was, from one cocktail too many. A real tragedy. I was riveted by his extraordinary playing. He looked and sounded like nothing on Earth — a powerful animal presence, almost as if he'd already died but had returned with increased supernatural power as the most animated zombie you'd ever see.

With that hair he could have been Medusa's twin brother stunning you not with his eyes but with his music.

His body melded with the guitar in a spellbinding dance of death. I loved him instantly. His death was no surprise. His songs seemed to have emerged from the bottom of the grave, deep in the ground. Like Jim Morrison, he was a natural born rider of many storms and I'm sure the real storm he played through at the festival was no coincidence… He was not quite of this Earth. Surely its most colourful visitor, and whilst like many I've had dreams of Hendrix, returning to pass on the occasional song.

Friend Gordon and I arrived on a splendid sunny day in idyllic conditions and enjoyed act after act. We hadn't remotely considered the weather might change. The necessity for a tent would have seemed like total overkill and would have been far too practical for the two of us. We were footloose and fancy free. Come nightfall it started to drizzle. We didn't even have a sleeping bag between us and there was no natural cover from the elements. We bought two large makeshift paper sleeping bags to cover ourselves. These things looked like giant jiffy bags and offered scant protection against the coming thunderstorm. We quickly became two sodden crestfallen individuals wandering around in a daze having given up the idea of sleep. Plus Richie Havens was on, sounding wonderful as thunder and lightning accompanied him like no earthly drummer. His god like voice seemed to rise straight out of the elements. He gave his all. I learned later that he hyperventilated after every show. He never held back, whether it was to a multitude or a small club. You always got 100% from the great man.

Music was becoming increasingly interesting, exciting and less predictable. I could feel the pulse of something that I couldn't quite put my finger on, just around the corner…

The road to finding Genesis was a five-year journey of ads and rejections in the back pages of *Melody Maker*, while I filled much of my time with various mind-numbing jobs. Though I harboured a dream of making a living in music I still had to survive financially.

A lovely pal of mine was a bass player, Archie, who'd rehearse with me at night. By day Archie worked at a local Labour Exchange, but by night he played the Astor Club. He offered to help me get a gig there, but I was too proud to accept. Kind though the offer was, I couldn't face the idea of wearing a penguin suit in a dance band, groaning through Engelbert's 'The Last Waltz' every night!

Ever the idealist, I held out. Initially, I worked for the Local Government Examinations Board, but I started to have nightmares about filing and the boss was a swine, so I left. I told the head honcho there that I couldn't stand it any longer, and he replied that I should realise all jobs are monotonous, but the *great* thing to find is varied monotony.

After this I was imprisoned in a printing factory for two years. The cacophony of the machines was less than musical and eventually threatened my sanity! Next came a solicitor's office next door to Old Scotland Yard. I carried a huge spliff through the courtyard of Old Scotland Yard to see if anyone would arrest me, but no-one did. You could walk through there easily in those days, and I also carried papers into the House of Commons. No security there either.

My favourite job was as a surveyor's assistant banging nails into roads, where my responsibility began and ended with each nail. It was a kind of industrial sleepwalking and I could happily dream away. The only eventful moment was when an ambulance nearly mowed me down as I was standing there dutifully in the middle of the road with my pole whilst the surveyor was getting a reading.

During my stint at the print factory I had to attend a business studies course once a week at the London College of Printing in Elephant and Castle. This could have been interminably boring but for meeting my life-long colourful pal Steve Tobin.

Whilst my destiny was to make records, his was to make commercials for TV. In those days he sported an afro with mutton chop whiskers, these days a suit with the occasional florescent bow tie, but he remains forever an original. I love him still for his forthrightness and stentorian voice — a born film director... "For God's sake Hackett, just fucking well get off your arse and get on with it!"

We had a blast. I showed up in some of his early films, prepared to do anything. On one occasion he asked me, did I mind being painted silver? I said, "righto!" and went to it with face paint and silver suit. I sometimes provided music for him too. His flatmate Jan Vogels also made films that involved me making a complete idiot of myself, cartwheeling about, busking, chasing a runaway umbrella... It was the 1960s after all!

Tobin has always been irrepressible. With his original take on life and never short of an opinion or two he still greets me with a healthy dose of insults — a natural choice of best man when Jo and I married.

It was Tobin who originally suggested I join a young band called Canterbury Glass. I did and duly sat in at a selection of strange gigs including a shotgun wedding at a working man's club. When relations soured between guests and band due to an impromptu freak-out session, the band were lucky to get away with their lives intact. "Don't shoot me, I'm only the harmonica player..."

There were distinct advantages to not being a fully-fledged member of the group. In the sixties it was very much anything goes, but it seems not so here. Amps were smashed, the police were called to separate the factions, when all that was needed was a milk white version of Engelbert Humperdinck's ever popular 'The Last Waltz'. For me it was a hair-raising moment and one of my worst memories of the semi-pro scene. The band members themselves were not without merit but very young and green (that well-known firm of lawyers).

I left Canterbury Glass but was very much on the look-out. I spent a great deal of time practising technique, but that wasn't enough to set the world alight without a band. In 1970 I joined Quiet World and enjoyed the experience of recording in a professional studio for the first time.

The band was headed by the three Heather brothers. They were English songwriters, but had spent many of their formative years in South Africa. Their father was a 'medium' who had ignited their interest in psychic phenomena, the supernatural and spiritualism. He influenced their song writing and would send tapes from South Africa to their flat in Bayswater, often speaking in his own voice but sometimes with the voice of apparently other discarnate souls. As we all sat round listening to those voices, I found it fascinating and became influenced in turn myself when he described music in pictorial terms. At one time for instance his words painted a picture of the ocean with a bird wheeling high above.

Some years later the guitar on 'Firth of Fifth' with its long-sustained note to introduce the theme was a chance to explore some of those ideas. A sustained note, a flight, repeat echo to conjure perspective, bending the note up and down to travel with the imagined flight of an elegant creature with mastery of its environment was the thing I had in mind. Fanciful yes, but a while later I became a member of the SAGB (Spiritualist Association of Great Britain) as a result of those tapes. I was intrigued to explore the whole idea of the spirit world.

Quiet World involved several interesting characters including the composer Phil Henderson who went on to write the *Far Pavilions* West End musical and master orchestral bass player Dick Driver.

Through Phil and Quiet World, I met Ian McDonald. Ian had been in the army learning music. A bum note could find you on a charge and require you to paint the grass green and the trees brown. Ian had co-founded the extraordinary early line up of King Crimson but had just left. I was already a fan of his multi-instrumental abilities and was chuffed to high heaven when he said he liked my guitar work. I was finally graduating beyond being a mere legend in my own bedroom.

I didn't spend long in Quiet World as we were ultimately heading along different lines and I needed to be part of a band which gave me more of a chance to give a personal contribution, but it had been a good experience, and I've remained pals with Phil Henderson and Dick Driver to this day. Phil continues with his music and lives in Haworth where the Brontë sisters wrote their iconic books.

On a day off from my recent tour celebrating forty years of *Wind & Wuthering*, it felt appropriate for my wife Jo and I to visit him and see the place which inspired *Wuthering Heights*. Phil showed us all the haunts on that extraordinary desolate moorland. Dick still plays with orchestras and often plays his double bass on my albums along with other great classical musicians he introduced me to… orchestral sounds joining the rock.

4

Jumping into space...

The need to stretch music beyond the confines of specific genres was already a strong driving force by 1970.

From the moment I left school for five years I kept an advert going in the music paper *Melody Maker*. In the early days it was "Blues guitarist / harmonica player seeks work" But then as I was introduced to new, innovative music my tastes and interest in music widened. I was becoming fascinated by the breadth of possibilities.

By 1970 my advert read "Guitarist writer seeks receptive musicians determined to strive beyond existing stagnant musical forms." It was a bold statement suggesting high expectations of both myself and anyone I was to work with, but it must have had the right tone, as it attracted the attention of another like-minded idealist.

It was one of those grey late Autumn days when I was back in my bedroom practising guitar licks, after helping Mum to take stuff out to the bin in the yard and dreaming of a rosy distant future, when the phone rang. "Hello, my name is Peter Gabriel. I've just read your ad…"

I remember my Genesis audition with Pete and Tony Banks, both showed up looking a bit like Tom Baker from *Dr Who* with long dark overcoats and woolly scarves. There

61

was Pete wearing his father's trousers and shoes. They'd embraced an anti-image approach. They both sounded posh and seemed different to most of the people I knew who tended to have that sharp edgy London vibe, unless they were stoned of course.

I hurtled through some pieces for Pete and Tony alone and with my brother John on things written for guitar and flute. I could also play a bit of blues with my harmonica whilst John strummed along. One of the numbers we touched on, 'The Hermit', was to appear later on *Voyage of the Acolyte*. I played both electric and acoustic guitar, and it helped that I also played twelve string. My love of all three kinds of guitar put me in very good stead with the guys. I think they liked my eclectic approach and my interest in all styles of music. Had I realised I was competing with about forty other guitarists I would have been a lot more nervous. It was probably a good job I was in blissful ignorance.

Pete did all the talking and Tony sat there silently, blank expression. It wasn't until six months later that Tony said, "I really liked what you played that day." I would never have known! But I appreciated the comment. It validated my contribution.

Pete said he enjoyed several of my ideas and recommended I listen to 'Stagnation', which the band was rightly proud of. I loved the song and the synchronicity with my advert's reference to stagnant music forms. I felt an affinity with Pete, and I sensed that in many ways we were on the same page.

But I was unsure whether I wanted to throw my lot in with a fully formed band from a completely different background and lifestyle to mine. Most of them were ex public school from well-off families in the heart of the idyllic English countryside with hopes that their children might one day rule the country, or at least quell a rebellion or two in a distant British colony. My background couldn't have been more different. I felt I'd sprouted up from a pavement crack in the centre of the urban Pimliconian jungle, that unpredictable, precarious world awash with pickpockets, bullies and bombsites... How could I fit in with their comfortable, self-assured club, and could I cope, spending weeks away from home with them to rehearse in a privileged country retreat? It all felt so alien. It was as if I'd just been offered a ticket to Mars... a terrifying prospect!

Becoming increasingly unsure, I mulled over all these thoughts on a long walk, and by the time I reached The World's End at the bottom of Kings Road, I somehow felt my own world had come to an end. Finally, a band with two albums already under its belt had approached me, but I didn't feel up to the challenge. Like a snail slipping back into its shell, I crawled in through the door of *The Last Resort* (the name my pals and I gave to the Chelsea Potter pub) to drown my anxieties in a beer or two. Leaving the sunshine outside behind, I felt comforted by clouds of cigarette smoke within the dark interior. Then I realised I wasn't alone... there was my friend Frank Murphy, coughing in a corner and looking as lost as myself. I bought two beers and headed in his direction.

I hoped he'd validate my decision and join me in a familiar alcohol-fuelled funk. It was a tradition with pals like Frank to grumble with blood-shot eyes in there for hours about not being able to afford anything or lament the loss of our latest loves.

But this time was different. He lifted his head and looked at me with a steely gaze... "You've heard of them, haven't you? You aren't doing anything better right now so why don't you join them?"

I desperately tried to find a lame excuse to avoid his challenge, but I realised he had me cornered. His words pierced the fog with sharp clarity.

Once again I was up against that invisible wall, aware that I had a choice either to sit there and give in, or to climb over it. But once over the wall, you can never go back. I knew there and then that I was about to take a leap of faith into that new world and that my life was about to change for good. I was about to board a spaceship to a new planet with a bunch of aliens. I emptied my glass, put it down and walked out through the door into the sunshine, clutching that ticket to Mars.

I knew Pete and Tony were happy for me to join the band, but they needed to ensure I got on with Mike Rutherford, "our other guitarist". Meeting Mike really did feel like coming face to face with a Martian, or at least a strange character from *Titus Groan*. He hadn't been well, and I met him while he was recovering. I remember he was in bed in his pyjamas. He sat up and greeted me, extending a long bony hand, whilst his low cultured voice and facial expressions resembled Christopher Lee. He was plainly a dark lord from another world. Yet, we immediately began to swap chord shapes and played off each other. There was a quickening in the air... As fellow musicians we formed a bond there and then. I was able to kick in with a new inversion of G major and the dye was cast for a continued working relationship.

Pete had a warmth about him, and I could tell that he was an original thinker. He and I immediately hit it off, and he kindly invited me to stay overnight with him. He was still living at home at that time. It gave us a chance to play one another records and get to know each other. I was finding a new niche, and the alien aspects were becoming more amusing than frightening.

I remember sitting at the family table with Pete and his father whilst his mother was preparing food. His father was an inventor and I observed him pondering some scientific conundrum. Embers from his pipe were falling on him and at one point his clothes caught fire. Very calmly and deftly, the mother picked up a leather apron conveniently placed close by and placed it over him. It just about covered the entire human body and dowsed the flames. I don't think Pete's father noticed. His mind was clearly elsewhere, trying to find the key to an insoluble equation.

I could see how Pete had inherited his father's innovative mind in several ways. He took preposterous risks onstage and his thinking was often bizarre. From the moment he put on that fox's head and his wife Jill's red dress, he started to depict album covers. He didn't just perform the songs, he lived them. He was a front man, prepared to wear anything to get Genesis on magazine covers. Songs such as 'Watcher of the Skies' only reached full potential live once Pete depicted the alien character in the story, influenced by Arthur C Clarke's *Childhood's End*. Pete had an actor's approach to a singer's performance and was a huge part of the band's rise to fame.

I'll always hold Pete in great affection for all sorts of reasons. He was the guy who got me into the band, giving me my first real break. We were both idealists, thinking of new ways of presenting the music. We'd often bounce wacky ideas off each other. I remember the first conversation we had where I suggested playing the guitar with a violin bow, making a shunting noise like a steam train in the dark before the lights came up.

Even after we'd both left Genesis we maintained a connection. I felt a strong affinity with Pete and his love of what was to become known as world music. In the 1980s I gave him a copy of my album *Till We Have Faces* because I knew he'd like its total immersion in rhythm. It impressed him sufficiently to want to record percussionists in South America himself.

Pete had eclectic tastes in music. He was a great fan of Nina Simone, the American band Spirit and Musique Concrete.

The other band members brought their own inspirations to the Genesis mix too.

Mike loved Joni Mitchell.

Tony particularly loved classical music. We'd discuss composers like Vaughan Williams and Tchaikovsky.

I feel that in many ways Tony had survived a privileged yet rigid background. Public (private) school is a system designed to produce captains of industry, with all the psychological pressure that entails. Tony joked that out of all his family he was the most easy-going. He was hugely talented and extremely competitive in equal measure. He now realises that I was an ally to him when I was a band member. I was keen to increase the keyboard arsenal to expand the talents of Tony who I still view as one of the greatest English composers. He was the most fluent chordsmith I'd ever met when I first joined 'the Regiment'.

He was a living contradiction. One minute he'd be furiously blowing his top and the next he would sit at the piano, creating the most exquisite ripples of sound. I always wanted to get to know him better and we did share a lot of good times and laughs, but he remained an enigma. I realised that to get the best out of him, it would have to be on his terms. As soon as he played anything interesting in rehearsal, I'd immediately suggest we use it. The band was hard to impress. Sometimes it was as tough as playing to a bunch of stern-faced Russian ice-skating judges... Even

Tony took a deep breath when auditioning a new idea.

Despite his detached exterior, Tony had a very sweet side. I remember one dark night in Glasgow when the five of us were driving along. In front of us a drunk guy attempted to cross the road, missed the curb and fell flat on his face. Tony was the first out of the car, ensuring the unfortunate fellow was okay. With Tony's help, this character was back on his feet in no time. Genesis would not have been the same without him. I'll always love Tony and his work.

I liked Phil Collins immediately when we met. He was the kind of character who seemed able to difuse atmospheres with a quick joke during tense rehearsal sessions. Already a pro, a veteran of theatre and film appearances, having performed many times as the Artful Dodger on stage in Lionel Bart's *Oliver*, he was easily the loudest drummer I'd ever encountered, playing until his hands blistered every night. He put everything into it. We shared a love of movies and often went to the cinema together. A particular favourite of his was Zefferelli's *Romeo and Juliet*, having once been up for the part alongside a girl he was particularly close to when they were still at stage school together.

Although he was a powerful rock drummer, his romantic side was to surface hugely over the years. I remember him surrounded by current and ex-girlfriends, always a hit with the ladies, whilst I struggled to overcome shyness, having dedicated myself solely to music for quite some time. I'd almost forgotten how to talk to girls at all and tended to be tongue-tied in their company. Later on, once the band had gained in stature, I'd gained in confidence with women to the point that Phil started to introduce me on stage as "Steve, lock up yer daughters Hackett"!

I remember spending time with Phil when he was listening to Mel Tormé singing with Buddy Rich and telling me that Big Band stuff was really where his heart was. Blues didn't really resonate with Genesis. I think that was more a guitarist's medium. At the time I didn't realise it but the seeds of what was to become progressive rock were being sown back in the day with Buddy Rich because there were so many accents in that music, where the bar seemed to arrive early. This was common to the approach of both Genesis and Yes. Bill Bruford was also a big fan of Buddy Rich. In Genesis there was a collision of influences from classical and church-based harmonies with big band energy along with folk music and rock. I loved the way that with their eclectic interests, just like me they wanted to avoid clichés.

Before I joined Genesis, I saw them at the Lyceum. I was impressed and I was aware I had a lot to learn to keep up with them, but I was aware there were ideas I could give them. The band just ambled into the first number and the song was acoustic. It had a nice twelve string section but didn't really go anywhere. I found both their presentation and some of the music too low energy for live performances.

I realised too that the stage could have a slicker look, less of a lash-up. It looked a bit like a raft caught in a storm! Towards the end of the show everything heated up with some heavier numbers, which showed their potential. I could see that with a harder edge including a more explosive guitar style, they had a real chance of cracking it. I knew I could help them acquire a dramatic dark edge. I was very keen that we should sound as loud and powerful as possible.

I also felt a Mellotron would add a whole new area of power. Having seen Crimson and The Moody Blues with one of these, I just knew it was a kind of Magic Minotaur, a powerful beast that if harnessed and used in the right hands was potentially an incredible weapon. I could see how Genesis would be able to fly back and forth in time on the back of this monster, which was also an extraordinary Pandora's box of tricks that I could tell would fit Genesis' idiosyncratic style and innovative song writing.

I was keen for us to have a light show and a synth as well as the Mellotron. I expressed all my thoughts, perhaps a bit undiplomatically as I wasn't used to working in a team. But they must have respected me as they didn't tell me to get lost! I realised that they needed me, as I needed them. I continued to suggest changes at different times, not always popular with the band but usually a good move.

In some ways my role was to be the one who'd take a look at the band as if I was an outsider. I liked to walk out front with a guitar and long lead at soundcheck to get an overview... to be on stage and off stage at the same time. In some ways I was the 'black sheep' outsider when I said unpopular things, but I feel I helped give perspective. Pete often understood what I was trying to do, and we sometimes formed a constructive alliance to pitch the band forward.

I realised that I was Ant Phillips' successor. He'd been the guitarist from the beginning with the band when they were still all at school together. I very much admired his playing and composing. His twelve-string work was exquisite. I was concerned that I wouldn't be able to match up to him in the eyes of the others. Ant has always been a lovely guy with a fantastic sense of humour as well as a fabulous musician and composer. Although we were never in the band together, he and I became friends and still are to this day. We've collaborated as well on more than one project. Now we're pals who can look back on the past together with fondness and amusement... and Ant is a guy with a fantastic sense of humour! But in those early Genesis days I felt constantly nervous, and it took a while to overcome that sense of social differences.

The first rehearsal with the guys was in West Hampstead. I realised I needed to learn not only the songs but also the Genesis lingo. They had strange words for several things like "guy" for a chord shape. "That's a nice guy," Mike would say. They had their own language and shared experiences which felt foreign to me. They had an air of reserve too, which often left me wondering what they were thinking. They were patient with me though, and Richard MacPhail who was always on hand to support us as close friend, roadie and in-house therapist was very reassuring. He said my attitude was right because I wanted to improve.

My little amp couldn't compete with Phil's drum kit, so I bought a loud, clean Highwatt stack. The band's music fascinated me. At this point, it was as much acoustic as electric, with elements of heavy rock in occasional bursts of frenzy.

The first concert I played with Genesis was at London University. There could be a cosmic link here with the fact that my own genesis in 1950 was in London University Hospital, and my wife Jo left home for the first time to study at the same university. All initiations into the university of life.

The London University gig was a baptism of fire. I wasn't used to doing live gigs at that stage, the material was new for me and there was so much to get right. I used a Rose Morris Shaftesbury Duofuzz. I couldn't stop it feeding back, which threw me, and I played so many bum notes. I wanted to crawl off the stage and die. I was convinced they were going to sack me.

But no one complained. Revelation… The aliens had sympathy! They could see what was going on and were giving me a new chance.

The next gig in Bangor, Wales, where The Beatles

had travelled to see the Maharishi, was a much easier experience. Very few people showed up but now I had a Marshall Superfuzz which worked, and I played sufficiently well to redeem myself. I was happy to get through it and I passed the test.

The third show at the Lyceum was terrifying, as it was such an important venue. My mother said I looked green! But I did okay, and the show was well attended. I was still so nervous that I forgot to walk off stage at the end and Richard had to lead me off! "It's over now Steve" he said with a gentle smile. Once I was backstage and normalising, I realised I'd passed the test. This was what I'd been building up to all these years and it was working!

The Six Bob Tour followed on straight after. It was a good move, the shows were well attended, often sold out, and my confidence began to improve. Charisma promoted three bands in town halls throughout the UK, Genesis, Lindisfarne and Van der Graff Generator.

The bus situation with these three bands of contrasting characters was pretty comical. The friendly down to earth Lindisfarne guys sprawled out in the back, beer drinking and singing songs. I particularly liked Ray Jackson (Jakko), who played mandolin on Rod Stewart's 'Maggie May'. Genesis sat in the middle in an insular bubble, either reading books or doing the Times crossword. In the front, observing the open road ahead, the Van der Graff Generator chaps would chat away about anything, from the price of bed sheets to the meaning of life and the secrets of the universe. Dave Jackson was particularly interesting to talk to. I enjoyed moving between all the guys in the bus, depending on whether I felt introverted, chatty or up for a few pints in the makeshift bar at the back!

Not only did the band characters contrast, but so did

the music. It felt odd to us having performed our complex music and songs such as 'The Musical Box', listening to Lindisfarne drumming up a storm with the audience all singing along... "We can have a wee wee, we can have a wet on the wall"! But to be fair on them, Lindisfarne's 'Lady Eleanor' with the touch of Edgar Allen Poe was magical. Van der Graff Generator had an interesting sound, but for me Genesis' music was more special, with so much variety and potential. I found that although initially I had one or two beers before a show to calm the nerves, I couldn't continue with the Lindisfarne approach because my playing suffered. From then on, I didn't drink anything until after the show.

Soon after the Six Bob Tour, Richard Branson gave us a free trial day to record the single 'Happy The Man' at his Manor Studio, Oxford. When it was time to leave, a scruffy looking guy with long hair and glasses gave us a lift to the station in the oldest banger imaginable. I assumed this chap was just part of the hippy help. Pete said afterwards, "I think that was Richard Branson himself" and indeed it was! He obviously employed the stealth approach, just low key, open and incredibly friendly. I saw him once or twice after that... he always seemed to be a man of the people. But obviously a shrewd operator. Extraordinary that he's now selling tickets for journeys into space, the most elite crowd funding venture dreamt up so far!

The closest I've been to Outer Space was on Concorde. On one night journey, I was invited into the cockpit which afforded an extraordinary view. It looked as if all of space surrounded me, the stars were so clear and I was literally looking at the moon way down below us. From that glass canopy, it had an altered perspective and we were flying so high, it felt like being a guest on the bridge of the Starship Enterprise...

Following 'Happy the Man', we began to plan for *Nursery Cryme*.

I felt Genesis really had the goods musically. There were still things that worried me though. It wasn't easy to start with being the support band of the support band at the time. With rambling story introductions and moments of musical meandering, we easily lost audience attention. Knowing Pete was a forward-thinking character, I appealed to him on the visuals, saying I felt we had to have a light show with a lighting designer who'd connect with our music. With a Mellotron too we could really be cutting edge.

When I heard that King Crimson were selling their Mellotron I jumped at the chance and Tony Banks and I went to meet Robert Fripp at a King Crimson rehearsal session in a dark, cave-like rehearsal facility in the bowels of a greasy spoon café. I was amazed to see that Crimson had four Mellotrons! Maybe it was because they were unreliable — both wonderful and terrible in equal measure... Condensation, sweat, being moved around... It was like a huge belligerent beast. Everything upset the Mellotron! But what an incredible beast it was — We could sound like an orchestra one minute and a rock band the next and eventually like a choir from all those tapes within.

Once we had the Mellotron we were able to do songs such as 'The Fountain Of Salmacis'. A combination of keyboard, Hammond organ and Mellotron together sounded magic. I was keen for us to get an RMI keyboard, which could sound like a harpsichord, but at other times an organ. All these things together added to that special Genesis sound where people often couldn't tell what the sound source was. Was it guitar, was it keyboard? It was very much a calling card of the band. Two instruments together could often make the sound of a third instrument. If you doubled a Hohner

Pianette put through a fuzz box trying to sound like a guitar with the guitarist trying to sound like a keyboard using the tapping technique you had something exciting that people couldn't pin down.

We fired off salvos at each other on tracks such as 'The Musical Box'. Here I used vari-speed, recording guitar at half speed to make it sound like a musical box. Working with sound colour was important to the band. Genesis' approach was often like an orchestra, at times very subtle but with the ensemble approach we could sound incredibly strong.

Now came my next Genesis baptism, which involved more than just music. While most of them had spent a lot of time away from home for years in public school, I'd never left home for any long period of time. We rehearsed *Nursery Cryme* in a building known as Toad Hall at Tony Stratton-Smith's (Strat's) place 'The Cottage' near Crowborough in Ashdown Forest, darkest Sussex.

My life completely changed when I joined Genesis. Now suddenly I was removed from my familiar Pimlico environment and transplanted into a large 'cottage' in the heart of the British countryside with a bunch of guys from a vastly different world to the one I knew. They were used to being away from home, most of them having lived together for years before in public school dormitories. With the exception of Phil Collins, they sounded very posh, and had their own codes.

On arrival at the Cottage, Mike immediately spied a book entitled *The Memoires of a Fox Hunting Man* and picked it up enthusiastically commenting, "Yes, that's a very interesting book actually...", whilst I sank uncomfortably into a large armchair. Like my pal Brian May, I've always actually loved foxes and have often fed them in the bleak mid-winter.

At night I'd wake at 3am, expecting to hear the comforting bell resounding loudly outside Victoria Station, but instead in that cottage, there'd be an interminable silence outside the pitch-black room. No traffic, no clanking trains to lull me to sleep and no streetlamps or flashing car headlights to guide the way to the bathroom. Then suddenly there was the incessant racket of birds tweeting away first thing in the morning. How was a guy supposed to sleep with that? Being the healthy soul that I was, I'd give up on sleep and head for my pack of cigarettes. A good smoke with my accompanying hacking cough was very grounding and a great source of comfort. I'm sure I woke everyone else up with that racket!

I don't think the other Genesis guys found me particularly suave and I don't blame them. I looked like a Polish dissident with a *Colombo* style raincoat which gave them the idea of the nickname "Hackett of the Yard". Even when I got it together to wear something more sartorial, I invariably ruined it. I remember on one occasion after an all-night mixing session, getting so tired that I fell asleep in a chair, spilling a mug of dark coffee over my new white trousers. Once again, a great source of amusement for the others!

But at the cottage, it was not just the strangeness of the place and company that made me feel lonely. When we weren't rehearsing, I became very aware of being a single guy, not just because I wasn't used to it, but while the others had girlfriends who either stayed or visited, I didn't. Barbara, Juliette, Sue... they had all gone their own ways. I didn't even keep much contact with friends at the time because all my energy was concentrated in one direction. In recent times I had exclusively devoted my life to music. The other band members sometimes wondered if I was gay. I didn't realise just how alone I felt until one night when I was talking to Peter's and Tony's girlfriends Jill and Margaret, and Jill said, "Don't you have a girlfriend Steve?" I burst into tears and left the room. I was too embarrassed to come back down and slept with my guitar.

It was different when we were rehearsing. I became absorbed by the music. I was aware that Phil and I were the new boys in the situation and it was often easier to get one person on board with an idea first, and then present it to a committee that had been together since childhood! But that was a means to an end and many great melodies were being worked on.

The arcane world of *Nursery Cryme* was full of unusual chord sequences and lyrical ideas were constantly surprising. No-one else sounded quite like it. As a detail freak, I was constantly analysing how sounds worked. I was keen to help bring out the best in everyone. I often encouraged Tony, who swiftly composed some extraordinary music.

I could always see how talented and original they all were, and I was thrilled to work with them. It was a truly creative period and the band flourished in this environment. At times it felt like a force of nature. It was a hot summer. We sometimes sat on the grass outside with twelve string guitars. Songs like 'Harlequin', 'For Absent Friends' and 'The Fountain of Salmacis' were born out of that summer. When we were on a real roll we'd continue indoors into the night.

I wrote the top melody line of 'For Absent Friends' and Phil and I wrote the lyrics. I felt we were writing our own 'Eleanor Rigby', with imagery like the abandoned swings symbolic of the harsh greyness of British life. In this little song was a direct thread to *Wind and Wuthering* with the sense of the bleak English landscape. This was Phil's first vocal contribution, which worked a treat. Many thought it was Pete singing. Extraordinary how there was a similarity, each of them to become a great rock singer in his own right.

I felt that 'The Fountain Of Salmacis' was a beautiful epic track. The Greek mythology lyrics were wonderfully evocative of the ancient world in all its mystery and passion. On one occasion we felt moved to go into the cottage late, and at midnight creative blocks came tumbling down as we started to play the end part of that song. A new kind of music was being born. A huge leap forward, my notes bending on top of Tony's beautiful chords on keyboards, sounding like orchestra with choir. It was pure spirit. All my emotions went into my guitar solo. I felt I was able to add significantly to the song's romance and wide range of extra colours. Once we recorded that track, the Mellotron's tidal waves of sound added yet another exciting dimension.

I worked furiously on guitar parts of 'The Musical Box' from the delicate tinkly interspersions to the huge elegiac finale. The guitar instrumentals on 'The Musical Box' were personally ground-breaking! My three-part harmony on that song, Brian May later claimed to be an influence on his playing. I used tapping too — the technique later explored by Eddie Van Halen amongst others. I also tapped on 'The Return of the Giant Hogweed'. Unfortunately, neighbours complained, which put a stop to the night sessions, but the magic had already been woven.

Richard MacPhail worked hard to take care of everyone. The strong young Viking look alike with long flaming red hair was actually one of the sweetest guys I've ever known. He constantly supported us and enabled us to concentrate on work. He was very positive and equally idealistic. Later on, he became deeply involved with green issues and eventually ran a successful alternative energy company. A man of many talents, who today runs his own hospital radio show.

During my time with everyone, I realised that the stiff "poshness" was only an aspect. The guys could behave as childishly as the rest of us, which was a revelation! I remember a journalist once joking that whilst members of The Who would happily trash a hotel room, Genesis would do no more than break a teacup, and even then, they'd own up to the hotel staff. But at times the differences were not so great...

On one occasion I remember Mike getting drunk and hurling wine glasses, smashing them around the room like a young Cossack at a sabre dance! The vibe at the cottage was often fun and it turned out to be a good, productive time for us all.

Once rehearsals were over, we spent a month at Trident Studios in central London to record the album. On release it received a mixed reception. Many loved it, but some knocked it. One critic suggested the lyrics had been unearthed from books. But I feel that if mythology touches you, whatever its root it links with personal feelings and experiences. The album might not have been hailed as a classic at first but was applauded in retrospect.

The *Nursery Cryme* gigs were played at all sorts of unlikely venues, from the end of the pier to the Dog & Duck pub and even the odd public school. The rough went with the smooth. I remember when we played Eton one of the young boys wanted me to sign his wing collar after the show. I was about to sign when an older boy butted in, "What are you doing out of your house, Watkins? Be off with you, quickly boy!" The youngster scurried off. Then the same imperious twit of a potential future prime minister turned his oily charm on me… "Would you mind awfully signing *my* wing collar?"

The response was always good when we played boys' schools. You can imagine the excitement from an all-male captive teenage audience when a rock band showed up to entertain them. They always went ballistic. Conversely, when we played Cheltenham Ladies College for girls, we were in for a shock. We were expecting them to swoon at the first power chord and we imagined they would hardly be able to contain themselves with a bunch of young guys such as our debonair young selves on stage. But how wrong could we be! They were the worst audience we ever played to. They just sat there, refusing to show any enthusiasm, probably terrified they'd be expelled if they so much as clapped, much less cheered. I could imagine they must have been severely warned… "Now girls, we've got a treat for you, a musical group. We're told some of them must have come from good families as the name Charterhouse was mentioned. But they are one of those bands. As soon as they've finished, you must all be back in your dormitories after prayers of course." Personally, I couldn't wait to get out of that privileged bastion of repression.

It was exhausting travelling many miles both day and night. On one occasion, our van crashed into oil drums on the motorway. One of them jammed under the front bumper, and we skidded for what felt like forever before slowing down. Sometimes, road disasters were totally out of our control. A short while later on the way to a show in Lyon in France, a guy pulled up sharp in front of the equipment van, which went straight into the back of his vehicle, and then the band coach promptly piled into the equipment van!

The first foreign shore we ventured out to was Belgium. It was my first time abroad with the band and the first place to fall under the Genesis spell. It's a small country with a big heart.

Initially there was a ferry ride. Bleary eyed and awash with no sleep, I wasn't prepared and lurched about the tub spilling my beer. On entering Brussels we didn't so much hit town as limp into it. We arrived in a cold misty deserted street at 6 am and fell into a hotel with a narrow staircase plus only one toilet at the end of a dark, dank corridor. Worse still, the place wasn't ready for us, so we were back out in the street. No sleep, no food, but alcohol was on tap. What a healthy time that was! The start of world travel was really run on extended hangover, fuelled up on beer and cigarettes. For those who like their sleep and regular meals, forget touring.

Belgians were welcoming and nerves were eventually soothed after gigs that were well received. Meals were sumptuous too and we were applauded. We were still in a deplorable state, like the walking wounded deprived of sleep and good sense, but we represented something exotic for the Belgians who responded to the complexity and imaginative nature of the music. A special link with Belgium has continued to this day.

When I recently took the *Genesis Revisited* show to Brussels, the audience spontaneously hummed along to the flute solo in 'Supper's Ready', bringing a tear to the eyes of many in an extraordinary way, including us on stage. The poignancy of it captured the nostalgia for those early years. Like the Belgians themselves, I'll always remember that first visit to Belgium with a great deal of warmth.

Then came the great adventure that was Italy. Italy was wonderfully exotic to us. The average Italian meal seemed like a fantastic feast. All those courses and fabulous fresh food with flowing wine. I felt the band lost that stiff upper lip aspect as we became honorary Latinos there. The more they responded to us, the more we relaxed. Italy was a great big Mama with welcoming open arms. If Italy's roots were in the ancient world, then our spirits sprang from the same soil. Ironically, our song 'The Fountain Of Salmacis' was banned on Italian radio for being "too sexy", but the fans loved it!

It was a strange rollercoaster of experience, an uncharted adventure, where one day we'd be hailed as heroes in front of a 3,000 strong crowd, the next we'd be entertaining just three men minus the dog. On one occasion we played in a football stadium where unfortunately the few stragglers who showed up were not allowed to sit on the grass and were completely outnumbered by the heavily sedated inmates of a psychiatric hospital bordering the pitch. Trapped behind a high metal fence, the poor souls just stared glassy eyed at our show. We felt about as welcome as a condom at the Vatican.

Italy was unpredictable and volatile, like the volcanoes smouldering in its landscape. But we were swiftly to move into a whole new league in Italy. Songs which had an epic, mythological feel caught the imagination of Italian fans, possibly because of their strong connection with history and an epic past, dating back to their ancient Roman ancestors.

Entering Rome felt like coming home. From the moment I stepped off the plane I could tell there was something tangible in the air. It was a magical, silent welcome where I felt past, present and future merging in an instant... standing on the edge of the ancient world and sensing I'd need to return time and time again.

Tony and I were both fans of the incomparable Respighi's 'Pines' and 'Fountains of Rome'. It feels like the city has seen it all, from the worst nightmares to the most serene dreams that rise up from every Roman fountain. It's long been a source of inspiration, especially for my acoustic albums. Nearby, the Tivoli Gardens host the most wonderful collection of water courses and fountains, which many years later I was able to enjoy with Jo on a beautiful summer's day after a tour.

From fountains to colonnades, from gigantic piazzas to dark archways, Rome enticed us to gaze at its grand vistas and into its labyrinth of narrow streets. It all linked to the imaginative atmosphere of our music. You could sense the spirit of those ancient myths which inspired so much of its art and culture.

We played the Piper Club that night, which all went swimmingly until in his enthusiasm Pete went on a small onstage rampage and accidentally kicked the lead out of my pedals. So, no guitar solo possible for the end of 'The Musical Box' that night! Pete apologised, but I understood. He'd been caught up in a Bacchantic frenzy, along with the hot-blooded audience.

A dynamic performer, Pete did get excited on stage, and around this era was his first attempt at body surfing. Unfortunately, people didn't realise what they were supposed to do. The waters parted and he fell to the ground, breaking his ankle. He continued to throw himself into the crowd at later shows, by which time people understood and caught him. This was visually impressive and generally worked out fine, except for the time security wouldn't let him backstage because they hadn't registered who he was!

During those years there were some unusually hairy incidents in Italy. Around the mid-seventies, particularly 1976/77, political unrest impacted on the shows. The audience tried to break in for free during several gigs. Riot police were on the scene, punters were getting hurt and sometimes the crew were under attack. At one point our tour manager Regis Boff had to wrestle a crowbar out of someone's hand as they were about to leap on to the stage.

Italy wasn't the only place where things turned explosive. On the "Lamb" tour in 1975 we found ourselves in a frightening situation in Cascais, Portugal. The government was about to be overthrown the following day and it was like a tinder box explosion! There was a riot outside the venue with guns and firecrackers going off and upturned army jeeps in the street. I heard there were fatalities. The gig had no stable power for equipment and it was oversold. Pyramids of people clambering over each other were dangerously close to the balconies. We even had a terrifying incident the following day on leaving. The pilot of our plane suddenly aborted the take-off and the plane skidded across the grass for what felt like forever. The Trickster was "out", and it felt as if danger was stalking us at every turn. Jill Gabriel was particularly freaked, as she'd had a premonition about it all.

The UK had its own share of dangerous moments too! In one of my earliest gigs with Genesis at a university (I think Leicester) a bunch of Hells Angels stood up in front of the stage, shouting out and throwing bottles. We found ourselves playing amidst showers of glass and smashed bottles. When Mike understandably stopped the show and threw down his bass, a guy mounted the stage and punched him, at which point we all hightailed off the stage!

We also had a particularly terrifying moment in Germany, which occurred at a venue I've often played at Loreley in the Roman amphitheatre originally re-constituted by Hitler in readiness to address the victorious multitude. Thankfully, this never happened, and it's now a successful rock venue... except for one occasion. The local police had erected a drug bust centre next to the stage and someone from the crowd set fire to it while we were playing. Flames started to engulf the stage and we had to make a swift exit. But the show must go on, and it did once the fire was doused!

My first German experience came straight after those first Italian shows. I recall the infamous Zoom Club in Frankfurt, a city otherwise known by some as "Little Chicago". This could have been another dangerous show, but luckily for us it went smoothly with no incident. Cookie, who owned the club, was later murdered. It was here that I met my first wife, Ellen. She was serving drinks behind the bar to help out a friend. Ellen worked for a promoter called Fritz Rau, once a roadie for Marlene Detrich. Strangely, there was a certain Marlene kind of look about Ellen.

Ellen had a challenging "come hither" way about her and I was drawn to her. I think I was intrigued to understand what was behind her facade. She and I started writing to each other, and I rented a flat so she could stay with me. It was my first real break with home, but it felt natural by this point as I'd already been away on tour so much. Ellen joined me almost immediately. It was a shame that as a welcoming treat I lavished a Pizza Express meal on her. She wasn't impressed. Sadly, she was no more taken with my other regular haunt, the Chelsea Kitchen in Kings Road. I was trying my best, but I hadn't yet ventured beyond pizza, fish and chips or spaghetti Bolognese, which in my book at the time was the height of luxury!

We didn't really get on at home either. Sometimes we'd have a laugh together, but then it would go wrong again. I kept thinking there must be a way to make it work and I wanted to do the gallant thing, so when her visa ran out, I suggested we marry. It was a mistake, but we were young, and I was naïve. I also didn't think things through properly, as music was taking up so much of my time and thoughts.

There were good aspects. Ellen's family were welcoming to me and her mother Ingeborg was always hospitable and friendly. I have a great memory of going with the family to see Beethoven's Ode to Joy in Offenbach. Later I played there with Genesis. Ingeborg lived in Hanau, close to Frankfurt in a picturesque region of Germany linked historically to the Brothers Grimm. With the old timber framed houses and forested hills, the area did have a magical feel. You could imagine a witch or living gargoyle might jump out at you from behind a tree or a princess might still be spellbound in castle turret close by.

Back home things became increasingly difficult, but there was one place where the pressure was off between Ellen and me. She liked to go out for a drink or five... We were at our best having a laugh over a beer together.

She sometimes joined me in the Speakeasy, St Margaret Street, W1. This was a favourite meeting place for the music industry. The soundtrack was invariably Pink Floyd's 'Eclipse' or Steely Dan's 'Do it Again'. To this day those tracks take me right back to that time. Dave Hitchcock, producer of *Foxtrot*, often met me there with his business partner Neil Slaven. Strat often held court there as well. They were a friendly crowd and we often babbled and boozed into the night. I sometimes bumped into the Crimson guys there, including John Wetton, Ian McDonald and Robert Fripp. We didn't just relax there. Business was invariably discussed over a drink and many ideas and deals were forged in this after-hours watering hole.

Charisma had offices above the Marquee, so the pub crawl often began there. Then we'd all move down the road to the La Chasse Club but inevitably we would finally fall into the Speakeasy, already somewhat inebriated!

One tremendous character who worked at the Speakeasy was Luigi, famous for having kicked out Jimi Hendrix, who'd wanted to jam there all night. "We've all got homes to go to…" were Luigi's marching orders. Here he was King. He ruled the restaurant. He never smiled. If you could get him to serve you, it was an honour. If you asked him what was on the menu, he'd always reply "Strogonoff". I met him again recently, not long before he died. It was a warm reunion and this time he cracked a smile, like an old Maffioso.

My sojourns at the Speakeasy weren't just for drinking. I effectively became the band's publicist, schmoozing with journalists, trying to talk them into doing features, bribing them with Vodka and Orange or Scotch and Coke…

Pete and I were two born hustlers. Whilst I worked the bars, he was sometimes late to rehearsals because he would be on the phone drumming up business. The band were often irritated by his apparent tardiness, but ultimately it was for the group's benefit.

5

In the circus of becoming…

I was never at home for long as there was always a fair chunk of touring, which was gaining momentum at that time.

By 1972 France was opening up for us. I was proud to play the Olympia in Paris. There was something special about the place. Maybe it was partly because I knew Edith Piaf had performed here and I felt her extraordinary spirit, especially in the artists' bar. I've always loved Piaf. There's the whole of France embodied in her voice, along with the war, sadness, poverty, compromise, the lady of the night's predicament, the sad client, enforced gaiety, but also a big heart longing for love. It was a voice that spoke for everyone, transcending its time and capturing so much of the human spirit.

The French responded to us in the way they'd once responded to Edith Piaf and Charles Aznavour. I think they loved the romance in our music, as well as the combination of melancholy and triumph. Within our music I feel there was that spirit of seizing a bad situation and being able to turn a depressed day around, fighting our inner demons and taking control of our lives. Even today I feel that great transformative spirit when we play 'Supper's Ready' live, and again in recent times it went down a storm in Paris.

Gigs in that city have always been amazing with fantastic audience reaction.

Other places in France which blazed for us were Lyon and Marseilles. Lyon was delightful to explore with a fab atmosphere along the river, and although Marseilles had a dangerous undercurrent, it was full of life with its hustle and bustle, like a French Naples. We noticed many wonderful buildings in France too. I often staggered out in the morning with just a packet of Gaulois cigarettes for company to look around. I remember wandering through Chartres Cathedral with its dark, spooky interior, beautiful edifice and uplifting spire. France had an atmosphere which intrigued and drew you in...

One of our gigs at that time was filmed and shown on French TV. Although we didn't have much of a light show then, there was a raw energy, a quickening of the spirit and we all had a visit where everything you go for, comes off. This show was at the Bataclan, Paris where in recent times the horrendous atrocity took place, with so many people killed by terrorists. I heard the news straight after playing a show in Washington DC. A chill shot down my spine, with my warm memories of the Bataclan shot to pieces. But there were many memorable gigs in Paris and the fantastic spirit of the French people.

I loved France — the cobbled streets, films, joie de vivre, wine and food, even though we stayed in a procession of dodgy hotels in those early days. In one Lilles hotel, at about 6am I woke to an extraordinary amount of banging and hammering. I peeked out of the room an hour later to see that the room across the hallway (including walls) had been destroyed by a sledgehammer! (Maybe that influenced Pete's later track of that name) Nearby, three or four guys were relaxing and laughing on their cigarette break, proud of having done their job. It was a big contrast with the posh hotels we later graduated to, including flunkies in white gloves under sparkling chandeliers.

From old Europe to the New World... it was later in 1972 when we made our first USA appearance. This was with String Driven Thing for a charity show at the Lincoln Center, New York City. We were terrified as we entered New York because we'd heard there had just been a gun battle in the Gorham Hotel where we were due to stay! I felt like a tiny ant in a *Batman* comic, huge buildings looming above, and there was that strange smoke rising from funnels and cracks in the ground. Smouldering beleaguered Manhattan looked and sounded like Gotham City meets Metropolis. It seemed impossible to sleep at night with omnipresent wailing sirens. NYC was inspiration for ideas that were to form *The Lamb Lies Down On Broadway*.

LA felt equally strange. At the time of *Selling England by the Pound* we stayed at the Tropicana, the cheapest motel in town where out of work actors rubbed shoulders with hungry rockers. It was Christmas but ninety degrees which was thrilling, although LA smog played hell with my lungs. I had the impression that LA had no centre, yet it existed in celluloid dreams, from the old-style romance of Clarke Gable and Vivien Leigh to the gritty setting for *Rebel Without A Cause*. LA was the town where every other person wanted to know if you were famous, where did you exist in the pecking order and why were you there? Success was and still is the LA religion.

The States was full of contradictions. You could feel the sense of opportunity in that "Land of the free" but there was also a price to pay. More than once we were strip searched by US customs, I guess because we fitted the visual bill of typical long-haired musicians, perfectly parodied later in *Spinal Tap*. That's not an experience I would recommend to anyone!

On one occasion, after customs found some residual illegal substance left by a previous band in the car we'd hired, we were taken off into separate rooms. The customs guys were confrontational and aggressive, challenging me with large dogs as I stood there without my clothes on. Then suddenly an alarm startled these jumpy characters who swiftly pulled out their guns and spun around wildly, nostrils flaring. They then ran out of the room, leaving me standing there for several minutes, stark naked and wondering if I'd come out alive. What mood were they going to be in when they returned? Eventually I heard the army of feet and the door swiftly opened… But luckily, now they had other concerns and told me to get dressed and leave.

You always had to watch your back, particularly in New York. In both 1974 and 1977 equipment was stolen at one venue and a ransom had to be paid to retrieve it! As the song goes, "If I can make it there, I can make it anywhere…" You had to want it badly.

But ultimately the States was rooting for us. Even on that first tour we felt excitement grow. In a couple of years, it was to open up for us in a big way like a Tequila Sunrise breaking into a Harvey Wallbanger.

Although we were on the up internationally, we continued to record on home turf in Monty Python's surreal cloth cap v top hat London.

I gained self-assurance on the second album I worked on with the band, *Foxtrot*. I was very proud of 'Can-Utility And The Coastliners', which gave me the confidence that I could write a typically Genesis tune myself! The others pitched in on the second half with the writing, and I loved that part too as it sounded like a storm at sea... the bass pedal holding the line with everything else swirling around it. A beautiful piece of music. It was hard to play live, and quickly became an abandoned shipwreck, but in recent times I resurrected it and Steven Wilson who sang on the *Genesis Revisited II* version told me it was his favourite song from *Foxtrot*.

My piece 'Horizons' worked well as a palate cleanser to 'Supper's Ready' with its reflective simplicity, and a sense of the sun coming out. I used an acoustic guitar put through a Leslie cabinet to give it a swirly Genesis sound. I aimed for the beauty of a short Tudor piece, but it was heavily influenced by Bach.

Before we had the synth, my guitar playing was the only way to bend a note, and I'd also make the sound of a trumpet on guitar. You hear that particularly on the weird and wonderful 'Supper's Ready', which for many is the definitive Genesis track. I was particularly keen for us to do something of that length — a real opus and challenge for all of us writers! Everyone was involved and we all had a chance to solo on this song. It also gave Pete the opportunity to depict the action of the songs, helping to bring them to life and adding to the magic. With a lead singer who was prepared to dress up in anything, including a fox's head with his wife's clothes or whatever the occasion demanded and not be shy about it was all to the good.

Both Pete and I insisted that 'Supper's Ready' needed all the bells and whistles to do it justice live… a light show, the Mellotron, sound effects like slamming doors, the cry of "All change!", Pete's costumes such as the flower headgear… everything that excited audiences. It helped the band to move into a whole new gear. The more risks taken, the better.

Strat totally loved the song from the first encounter.

He was bowled over by the whole album, which he said showed the breadth of the band's work in an extraordinary way… From light and quirky to dark and imaginative… The futuristic 'Watcher of the Skies' had enormous power, whilst the social comment on 'Get 'Em Out by Friday' took another turn. Pete's social concerns showed through. He always cared about equality and believed in the idea that everyone should have a share of the world's goods. He extended this philosophy towards a band run as a democracy, everybody as respected writer.

The time of *Selling England by the Pound* was when I was at my happiest in the band. With three albums to draw on and a killer show, I knew we were doing the right thing with that album. There was both internal and external energy. I felt confident enough by now to come up with as many guitar riffs as possible. The band's first hit song 'I Know What I Like' was based on a riff I played with Phil, who had a way of really making it swing. It was the previous year's reject, and now it flew. It's always worked live, and these days when I play it with my band, Rob Townsend on sax gives it a whole new lease of life.

The rest of the album often has an elegiac feel. This is particularly true of my favourite track, which for me epitomises Genesis at its best, 'Dancing With The Moonlit Knight'. It begins with the magic and primitive feel of Scottish plainsong and sweeps through the anthemic Elgarian English melody with a choir that conjures the bygone Baroque age before revving up as it pitches ever faster forth via a flight through time into a wild fusion of sound. It runs the gauntlet of styles and is like musical time lapse… clouds fly by, flowers grow faster but also decay before your eyes, the old-world passes, giving way to the new urban concrete jungle — angular, detached, disconnected and cubist. By the end it's practically post holocaust. The end conjures water to me... an ultimate tranquillity beyond the maelstrom in the remnants of civilisation, the flotsam-&-jetsam of it all. There's something of Mozart's 'Requiem' in it — the loss of the personal touch in favour of big business and the sense that every civilisation must pass. It encapsulates the repeated theme in Genesis of the passing of time, and the memory of an era high on chivalry. It was an amazing hybrid between classical and rock. I don't think that any other band has written anything quite like it. It was a quantum leap forward for us.

Another standout track on the album, 'Firth of Fifth', was spearheaded by Tony, and he wrote the melody line which ended up being arguably my most iconic Genesis guitar solo. On keyboard I thought it sounded a bit sketchy, but I felt its potential and tried it on my trusty Gold Top Les Paul. I had the image in mind of a bird flying high above a calm sea. I altered the melody and bent notes to give extra emotional resonance which had the effect of sounding slightly Eastern, bringing out the epic nature of the melody again with an orchestral feel. Many have always found this solo hugely moving and I feel that playing slowly over strong bass and drums can be very powerful.

I was enraptured on stage during the *Selling England* tour. By now it felt like I was playing guitar in the greatest band in the world. It was also the year that John Lennon expressed his interest in Genesis, which boosted my confidence level no end. We had three amazing *Selling England* gigs at the Roxy in LA. US audiences were incredible. I felt more at home on the stage at that time than anywhere else. Once again, my life held that strange contradiction. My personal life was in tatters but by contrast the band was doing fantastic music and gaining momentum with increasing popularity as a bonus.

This tour also provided opportunities to meet other musicians on the road, such as the Focus guys. I saw their show and told Jan Akkerman that I thought he played marvellously. He replied that he felt he played like shit! Musicians can be incredibly self-critical, including myself at times. I still connect with Thijs van Leer today, who rightly has great self-confidence. He even plays his flute like the Pied Piper in virtually any situation, including the street, beach, café, you name it… bringing a party atmosphere and a smile to crowds both on and off stage.

Conversely, Robert Fripp who I also met during the time of *Selling England*, always appears to have had a schoolmasterly approach to both music and conversation. At a dinner party, he reprimanded me for eating too much of his cheese. To his displeasure, I ate another piece. I disgraced myself! Forty years on, I've never been invited back. But I continue to admire and respect Robert and the other Crimson boys for their amazing creations in 1969 and their tenacity to this day. They were leading lights in that pan-genre exploratory musical movement which opened up the way for so many of us.

Once the *Selling England* tour was over, I swiftly plunged from aspiring guitar hero into the role of downtrodden husband with Ellen and newly born son Oliver. Ellen found it hard to cope with taking care of a child. Most of the time I was changing nappies, feeding the baby and getting up at night to check on him. I can picture myself in my dodgy platform shoes, long hair and bedraggled handle-bar moustache pushing a pram down the street each day! The reason Ellen and I subsequently split though was not the pressure of parenthood, but because whatever I did, I could never make her happy. She was always angry and unable to deal with negative things which had impacted on her as a child.

After I left, Oliver was taken to Germany and brought up by Ellen's mother. I felt horribly guilty that I'd let him down. But I knew it was impossible for Ellen and me to carry on. I was glad to see he was in safe hands. I ensured he had financial support and visited him throughout his childhood. I continued to stay in touch with Oliver as much as possible once he'd grown up, and over the years I've kept an open line and it's good to see him.

It was never long before new challenges were afoot with the good ship Genesis. We decided to write and rehearse our next album at a former workhouse in the Hampshire countryside. I think the band hoped it might have a similar feel to Strat's cottage where we enjoyed doing *Nursery Cryme*, but Headley Grange turned out to be a different experience.

Once we were there, we realised the degree to which things had changed over the course of a couple of years. Phil and Pete now had family ties and I had the pressure of my marriage breaking up with a young child involved. Life had been relatively simple before, but we were all now growing, expanding and evolving into adult lives. Pete was particularly worried. He was seriously considering leaving the band so he could follow his own path freely, as well as giving his family more time. I was heartbroken about the potential consequences of losing him, but ultimately, we all understood and appreciated his commitment to seeing *The Lamb Lies Down On Broadway* through recording and touring.

In a sense, being away in the country was a refuge for me because of my split from Ellen, but Headley Grange was so run down that it hardly felt welcoming. You could feel those sad spirits of its grim past when you touched the cold walls. It was reputed to be haunted. I heard peculiar sounds of scratching and hissing at night. One weird and freaky thing that happened was an occasion when I'd just washed my hands in a bathroom. The second I stepped back from the basin, the floor gave way on the exact spot where my feet had just been, leaving a gaping hole. Robert Plant later told me he was convinced the place was haunted and Jimmy Page has claimed he saw an apparition at the top of the stairs when Led Zep were recording there, just outside the room where I slept. They'd picked up on the atmosphere in the place, particularly the elemental drum sound recorded in the creaky wooden stairwell for 'Kashmir', a piece of music that inspired all of us in Genesis.

I think some places are haunted, by what exactly I don't know, but I have had other strange experiences. In the apartment Jo and I first shared, objects moved inexplicably overnight. Sometimes a strong smell came and went with no connection to anything or anyone. Once I remember Jo and I when in the car in the middle of nowhere with no-one about, there was suddenly an incredibly strong aroma of dope. It stayed for about a minute and then swiftly disappeared. I smiled and said, "Could that have been Chris?" A day later, Chris Squire's widow Scotty called to say she'd just seen a medium who told her that Chris was trying to get through to me.

Recently, I saw an apparition for the first time. We were chatting over a cup of tea with pals in a modern house, and suddenly I noticed a man pass through across the kitchen and disappear through the wall. He was wearing old fashioned clothing and some kind of large cloth hat. So, who knows? A dead person? An imprint from the past or a glitch in time? Even scientists studying quantum physics no longer dismiss the apparently paranormal.

But whether or not spirits were haunting the hallways of Headley Grange, we all rode waves of inspiration there as *The Lamb* began to take shape. Pete wrote lyrics whilst the rest of us concentrated on the musical ideas. Phil became deft at switching on his cassette recorder with a drumstick! There are certainly haunting moments in *The Lamb* as in 'The Lamia' and 'Broadway Melody of 1974' which were influenced by the bleak, melancholic atmosphere of the Grange.

We recorded in remote Gaspant, Wales, followed by London's Island Studios, Basing Street. My two favourite pieces from it definitely are 'The Lamia' and 'Fly on a Windshield'. With 'Fly' we were influenced by the 'ramming speed' scene in the film *Ben Hur*... the march of death to accompany the suffering of a million ancient slaves. I wanted the guitar to sound like distant cries — the death agonies of prisoners. Then the triumphant chord change, as in Ravel's 'Bolero', with a victorious sense of a shift into a new dimension, at once beyond good and evil... When nowadays I play that piece of music, it's because of its timeless power.

At one point, from Phil's recommendation Brian Eno provided some electronic enhancements on vocal and guitar parts. An enthusiastic character, he was very into his boxes of tricks. In other words, a fellow experimenter, articulate with no previous band baggage. This left him able to influence us untethered in freelance fashion. He was a breath of fresh air and on that one session he helped to sharpen the edge for which *The Lamb* is still remembered to this day.

We were writing and recording at high intensity. *The Lamb* is a dense album with tons of detail. Everyone brimming over with ideas, the record was as packed with themes as Times Square is filled with people on a busy night, vocals suddenly abrasive like the horn of a New York fire truck. Forget sweet dreams… the drama unfolds day and night.

The Lamb felt like a titanic adventure we were trying to survive... and certainly it was like that for me. We struck icebergs, but bravely lurched on into shark infested, uncharted waters.

With my recent marriage break up and my feelings of guilt over the child involved, I wasn't sure what the future held. It was a very difficult time to find my way through to a new relationship. After leaving Ellen with the discomfort of the baby involved, my confidence took a dive and my spirits were low. I went back to living in my parents' small Pimlico flat. I appreciated Mum and Dad's support and it was good to be back with them and John too, but I felt I'd failed and taken a step backwards by sinking back into the adolescent environment. Knowing that Pete was planning to leave the band increased my anxiety further, and I knew I was going to miss him like a brother. He was such a lovely guy and we'd achieved so many great highs and dreams together. I knew the balance within the band was going to be harder to handle after Pete's departure. Also, none of us knew at that time if the band would continue to survive. He was after all the star of the band.

At that time the band's saviour and manager Tony Smith shared a partnership with Michael Alfandary and Harvey Goldsmith. Michael was currently promoting the Sensational Alex Harvey Band and invited me to their show at the London Palladium. The band lived up to their name and it was an extraordinary gig. Alex was a particularly great showman. At the after-show party in the Royal Garden Hotel, Kensington I heard someone say the band would be nothing without Alex. I immediately drew the parallel with Pete and Genesis. My hand tensed on the wine glass I held. The next thing I knew I was being rushed off to hospital. I'd severed a tendon and a nerve. I was given stitches to save my thumb.

The band still hadn't finished the album, so my injury gave a good reason to delay the *Lamb* tour. I was furious with myself and it was the first and last time I ever let anything emotional potentially get in the way of my work again. This was a turning point for me. A need for self-reliance kicked in and the idea of recording my own album took hold. But I was emotionally on a knife edge.

During the period of the *Lamb* tour I continued to go through my own version of the underworld journey, fighting for answers and struggling with old fears. I believe when you're in emotional turmoil, strange things start to happen. It's as if you attract the weird. Early on the *Lamb* tour Phil and I went to see *The Exorcist*. Normally horror movies have never phased me, but this one did as events later that day were downright freaky. A girl who'd once been a flatmate's partner showed up that evening with an enormous foam bunny rabbit for baby Oliver. She and I had never had any kind of relationship, but she was giving me a strange fixated drug-dilated look. Later that night when I was in bed she'd somehow found out my room number and started to hammer and kick on the door, shouting my name and demanding to be let in. Her screams swiftly rose to fever pitch as she pounded away with increasing ferocity, whilst the shadow of the giant bunny across the room visibly appeared to shake, looming ominously in a sequel to the horror movie. This demonic giant rabbit combined with deranged banshee, green foam no doubt spewing from her mouth, would have made a fabulous black comedy. But whilst I was having daily electric shock treatment to get my thumb working, at the time it was hard to be humorous and to find a calm centre! However lonely I felt, this crazed heroin addict was too much to take on, and I held out for an hour hoping that the door's lock would hold up until finally the screams and banging subsided.

Despite the night terror zone both real and imagined, I threw myself into work. It was going swimmingly with terrific crowds, but the moment I stepped off the stage I felt alone. I was anxious not to commit to another relationship in a hurry, but I became susceptible to the encouraging smiles of girls met on the road. Groupies were a reality.

These women were more in evidence at that time, as we were by then a successful band. They showed up mainly in the United States. The US was groupie central for a young English band. Needing companionship, a port in the storm and essentially searching for love, I responded. They courted venues, clubs and hotels. You could tell the intention in a look. It was a brave new world short on wooing and commitment, but there was this other kind of show which danced on into the early hours. There were some pretty strange encounters of another kind. I had brief involvements with several, from the burlesque dancer and the female wrestling champion to the girl whose fantasy was a brutal night with Vincent Price.

The passing ships in the night soon left me with an even deeper feeling of emptiness. I felt more comfortable with girls that wanted to converse and share their thoughts. The only occasion I ever paid a prostitute was literally just to talk. I invited her to have breakfast with me in a cafe. She was happy to be paid for the conversation and it helped me to bring up anything from music to the meaning of life with a complete stranger. I said, "It must be unusual, a guy just wanting to chat", to which she replied, "As a matter of fact, you're one of the normal ones." I wondered how she coped with her life, and I thought of the daily dangers she faced. She told me she did that job to support her young son. The encounter haunted me and later influenced the lyrics of 'Many Sides to the Night' on *Guitar Noir*. In the song I just changed the setting from the States to the UK.

Increasingly, I hoped that at some point a relationship would emerge. When the opportunity presented, I'd invite someone out for a drink or to a show. But the band was on the move all the time, so it was hard to strike up a relationship.

The girls I met loved an English accent. I was aware that any guy from an up and coming rock band would fit the bill. I think along with other musicians I fulfilled a fantasy for them. Those I met often mentioned other musicians they'd been involved with. I had the impression that most were trying to clock up as many musos as possible. Several of them talked about their previous involvements with musical heroes. I wondered if any of them would have been interested in me had I not been linked to a famous band. I remember on one occasion, a girl I'd just met shouting out at an inappropriate moment, "A Genesis in my bed!" So, there it was. I'd become "A Genesis". It didn't do my personal confidence much good and it equally confirmed where the girl was at.

My judgement was somewhat cloudy at the time... I was clinging to the occasional self-help book. It was hard to make rational decisions. I looked to strong-minded, self-assured people who I thought might lead the way, whether they'd take me on a trip up the garden path or not. The rigors of the road made me more susceptible to quasi cosmic clues and answers. I felt like a battered ship lost in a storm.

I was pretty spaced out by the time Genesis reached

New York in December 1974. I met Kim Poor after the show when she came backstage. I was talking to a girl I knew, and Kim entered the conversation. Then she and a friend of hers joined the band in the limo as we were about to leave. Kim had the glamour and self-confidence that I lacked at the time. I was smitten.

The beginning of the relationship involved a new adventure. With a plan to meet Kim and her family in her home country of Brazil for Christmas, I spent a couple of days with our tour manager Regis Boff in Miami before flying out. He jokingly said that he'd be surprised if I came back alive and I wondered what could be so dangerous there?

On my arrival in Rio I was bleary-eyed after a long flight and hadn't a clue what to do, but I needed to find a car to take me to the town of Petropolis up in the mountains where Kim's family lived during the hot season. A guy approached me, offering a cab. He was a dead ringer for Manuel from the British sit-com *Fawlty Towers*! His little cab looked like it had seen much better days, but at least this was transport. On the drive I noticed he appeared to have no operational brakes and drove the whole journey in one gear. It was a perilous road spiralling up a mountainside. I thought to myself, "This looks just like a Hitchcock movie ride!" as the car swerved around people carrying bananas on their heads and lurched away from the edge of the road above a sheer drop into a chasm beneath the mountain. I believed every bend in the road was about to be my last. Regis' words echoed in my ears and I was already envisaging a wooden cross overlooking the precipice, marking the place of my tragic demise...

It took an hour for us to reach Petropolis, by which time my face must have turned green. Eventually the car screeched to a halt, literally spewing clouds of smoke outside the gates to the family house. As I fell out of that death trap, my legs nearly gave way. I've never before or since had such a terrifying journey!

I appreciated the exotica of Brazil with its lush vegetation, beautiful mountains and magnificent coastline, but it was the land of infernal honey. The huge gap between rich and poor and the tough living conditions many people clearly suffered out there was disturbing. It upset me to see the cramped shanty towns clinging to hillsides and many struggling beggars on the streets.

Brazil also possessed a stranger kind of underworld. As I was already working on plans for my first solo album which involved the Tarot as a theme, I was interested by anything supernatural, so I was intrigued to meet a woman who claimed to have a connection to the spirit world.

A dark corridor led into a small incense filled dimly lit room adorned with strange combinations of ancient gods and Catholic saints with offerings. Sitting in the middle was this large, masculine looking woman with wild eyes smoking a cigar. She claimed to receive the spirit of Papagayu, apparently a pipe smoking male spirit. I guess he must also have been partial to cigars! She told me that the music I did was linked to some harp playing entity from over two thousand years ago. This intrigued and drew me in, but then she asked me to write names on pieces of paper. She set fire to one of them and the others she told me to put into my shoe and walk on them until they disintegrated. At that juncture I felt uncomfortable. I was glad to get away and I took the papers out of my shoe at the first opportunity! I realise this was the Brazilian practice known as Macumba, related to voodoo. I was spooked and relieved not to see her again.

Other aspects of Brazilian spirituality were more fun, like a ritual to celebrate the goddess of the sea Yemanja, where a boat of offerings was launched into the ocean at New Year. The changing tide, the passing of the old year, the hopes for the future…

The period of the *Lamb* project was indeed a strange period of change, a time of conflicting emotions, dealing with many beginnings and endings. Not only was there my marriage break-up and the start of another relationship, but the birth of my son was followed by the death of my grandmother's second husband who I knew as Uncle Charlie. He was such a warm character, full of life, inspiring stories and welcoming smiles. I'd always loved him since early childhood. It was very hard to lose him, and particularly difficult not to be able to join the family at that time and attend the funeral because of being away on tour.

Then all of us in the band had to come to terms with Pete's decision to leave and we were facing the problem that the band might not survive his departure. That feeling of insecurity was also one of the spurs driving me to start something new…

6

Pleasure Island was an overcrowded place...

L ong before the *Lamb* tour began, I was developing musical phrases and lyrics for a solo album. I was brimming over with musical ideas that I was unable to communicate, whilst internal frustration was growing under the surface. By 1974 I'd been involved with writing a lot of music for the band, but many of my own ideas had yet to see the light of day. Even though I'd just split up with Ellen and was deeply depressed, my inner musical world continued to thrive. It was both a haven and a creative spur. I felt a need to work beyond the constraints of the band but many of my own ideas were more romantic than the *Lamb*. I loved much of the *Lamb*, but personal ideas were beginning to knock on my inner door. As we were recording 'In The Cage' I realised my own musical ideas were fighting and dying to be let out of a similar cage.

A watershed time came towards the end of the *Lamb* recording. After the wine glass incident, the waters broke, and I realised I had to find a route to rebuild self-confidence. By the time I came out of hospital after the hand operation I was determined to embark on a solo musical voyage whilst remaining a band member. With ideas already brewing, I knew I needed to make my mark as an individual. I felt a new style of music incubating like a breath of fresh air. All was taking shape.

I was starting to use many sounds that although recorded for the *Lamb*, couldn't be heard properly on the original mix of the record. I wanted to explore these further, including the use of the synthi hi-fli, which produced a very wide vibrato effect. You can hear this with frightening atmosphere on 'A Tower Struck Down'. I had the band's mellotron at home and I started to write with the string sound and sketch out what was to become 'Hands Of The Priestess' and the first half of 'Shadow Of The Hierophant'. The big romantic sound at the beginning was written on the Mellotron. I was keen to do an album that would make full use of the world of malevolent mellotron. Every chord I played on it felt instantly magical and powerful.

My brother John was already a fab flute player and I knew we had great alchemy together. I had him very much in mind for some of the recently written melody lines, particularly with the piece that was to evolve into 'Hands Of The Priestess'. I'd already written the oboe melody for 'The Hermit', which John and I had played together to Tony and Pete for my Genesis audition.

By the beginning of the *Lamb* tour I was starting to experiment with writing both top and bass lines together. I wanted to create an instrumental track full of changes and using Mellotron voices. I mapped out the idea of employing electric guitars in octaves and in harmony. A whole world of possibilities was revealing itself, starting as a trickle and becoming a flood. Once I'd opened Pandora's Box there was no stopping me. During the tour, the ideas continued to germinate.

By the time the tour ended I'd amassed enough

ideas to form a whole solo album. I ran the idea by Tony Smith who was keen for me to go for it. I was hot to trot and immediately prepared to record.

I lined up several musicians and singers. I loved the sound of Sally Oldfield's voice in the folk duo The Sallyangie (with her brother Mike) which reminded me of Marianne Faithful — that seductive fast vibrato I so loved in other female singers too like Buffy Sainte-Marie and Edith Piaf. I tracked Sally down and ran the idea of 'Shadow Of The Hierophant' by her. Her brother Mike was more in the limelight at that time, but it was her voice I was interested in and she luckily seemed happy to be asked. She was later to have much deserved solo success.

Phil and Mike agreed to play on the album. Phil's Chinese cymbal played backwards to herald 'A Tower Struck Down' sounded like a demented pterodactyl on the loose. He also sounded great singing on 'Star Of Sirius'. It felt fantastic to record with brother John too, making his own stunning debut on this first collaboration between two brothers who had finally come of age.

This was also my first solo project with engineer John Acock who produced some brilliant sounds. Both of us played Mellotron, whilst John played synth as well as his flute. I was also using autoharp, harmonium and orchestron (string synthesiser). With the mixture of rock and orchestral instruments I felt like a kid let loose in a toy shop, and some fascinating sounds came out of "those toys from the attic".

At that time Mum, Dad, John and I were all living together in this tiny flat, but it was a powerhouse of creativity with two brothers rehearsing in the bedroom and Dad painting the world in the living room. Extraordinary dreams were born and nurtured in that place with Mum keeping the whole ship afloat.

Whilst recording my album, I'd stagger back into the flat each night at the ungodly hour of 3am, exhausted but thrilled, fulfilled and ready to write more. We were recording in a studio beneath Aviation House in Kingsway, London, where Fleetwood Mac had created much of their early material with Peter Green. When they were recording 'Green Manalishi' they used the car park as an echo chamber with PA for Peter Green to sing through. This was in the middle of the night. Unfortunately, no-one had told the night watchman, who was totally spooked at the sound of the ghost-like strains of Green's howling voice. Luckily for the night watchman we recorded 'A Tower Stuck Down' inside the studio!

'Hands Of The Priestess Part 1' was the first track to go to tape. A stunning debut for John's flute. By the end of the first night we had practically the whole of it in the can, it had gone so well! Each time we did a track I was thrilled to see it take shape. I was coming into my own and relished the whole process. The album sprang to life swiftly and gave me so much back. The record company were pleased and totally supportive.

Strat suggested the title *Voyage of the Acolyte*. The concept of the album which I came up with reflected my interest in the tarot. Strat said he'd heard the tarot cards were the devil's picture book, but I felt the approach I had with those cards was more like the Chinese I Ching or an ancient oracle.

The opening track 'Ace Of Wands' represents a new venture, which is exactly what the album stood for, and subsequently given the great response and its success, I did indeed feel I'd scored an ace with it! The image of the 'Priestess' personified the oracular power of the tarot itself as well as gentle feminine grace and the spirit of peace.

By contrast, 'A Tower Struck Down' gave me the opportunity to let rip with primal energies, screaming to be let out along with the horror of unstoppable forces running riot. I chose 'The Hermit' because I'd gone through a ton of hermit-like soul searching as I came up with this album. This song was also my first chance to take lead vocal. I chose 'The Lovers' as a counterpoint to 'The Hermit'. It's the instrumental melody of 'The Hermit' reversed. I felt the album needed a positive, light balance. 'The Star' represents renewal and reflection as well as a water bearer as in my own star sign Aquarius. As a card of hope it linked to my wishes for the future.

'Shadow Of The Hierophant' with its contrasting energies symbolised both shadow and light in the ancient world and its healing mysteries. It had an aspect of Greek Tragedy about it as in the Oresteia, with its strange hybrid of ritual, oppression and triumph with the processional feel of a musical crescendo. The end part of this song had already been rehearsed for *Foxtrot*. The eventual piece was a co-write between Mike and yours truly, which gave the album a rousing send-off. It was the album at its most orchestral in spirit, even though played by a rock band. The whole record was like a musical journey, ending with an overwhelming sense of empowerment plus a dream achieved. It was in a way a version of the group, but without having to answer to the committee.

As my first solo record *Voyage of the Acolyte* was a watershed album. I was both nervous and excited. With influences ranging from folk to rock, from jazz to classical, a pan-genre approach was adopted from the outset. It's all the more poignant now to think back on it all, with the passing of John Acock, Robin Miller and John Gustafson, all of whom were involved. It makes this musical memory all the sweeter — an unrepeatable point in time, a confluence of magical moments... a hot summer, a hot band, a nervous guitarist (me) hovering over unfinished tapes like a chain-smoking expectant father.

It was a liberating feeling to complete the project and a real sense of achievement. People were complimentary about the album. Pete Gabriel made some very positive comments about it which I appreciated.

As soon as I finished mixing *Acolyte,* I joined the other Genesis guys for *A Trick of the Tail.* Contrary to myth, I believe I only missed a day. I caught up quickly and joined the band for 'Dance on a Volcano'. On the beginning of the song we all managed to hit the same accents as if by telepathy. I wrote the fast and furious part. I enjoyed working on the album. The main melody for 'Los Endos' was mine. Phil came up with the furious rhythm to propel it beyond my dream. I've always loved the combination of slow, memorable melodies with fast rhythms and this track caught fire from the word go.

But I felt just as moved by the beautiful and gentle songs. I loved 'Ripples'. I wrote the guitar melody I played in the middle section and I created the melody for the verses of 'Entangled', whilst Tony wrote the 'chorus' part. The words were mine. I thought Phil sounded spectacular on it and he delivered a great three-part harmony.

I was thrilled to see Phil sounding so brilliant in his new lead singer role. I'd been very sad and disappointed when Pete left and I continued to miss him not just as a friend but as an ally in experimental areas. There was also the question of who could replace him as a singer. I believed Phil would be a natural choice, and indeed Jon Anderson of Yes suggested Phil as lead singer when I met him at Phil's first wedding.

Genesis auditioned several singers whilst rehearsing for *A Trick of the Tail*, but no-one was right. I even went with Tony Smith to see a guy singing in Jesus Christ Superstar, but the vibe didn't fit and we were so bored by the show that we left in the middle! Eventually Phil suggested having a go. Once he got to grips with 'Squonk', he just sounded so good that a star was born there and then...

I felt once we'd completed the album, Genesis was again a force to be reckoned with as a four piece. Years later I discovered from Chris Squire that he considered *Trick* to be his favourite Genesis album.

It was reassuring to have Bill Bruford, drumming demon of Yes and King Crimson, join us for the tour, but the band was understandably nervous about touring without Pete for the first time. I remember the first gig in Hamilton, Ontario. It didn't help that one guy dressed up like Pete in batwings stood near the stage for the whole gig, but Phil came through. He was obviously a terrific front man from the word go. He impressively covered both vocals and, along with Bill, drums. Phil was theatrical, but in a more earthy way than Pete. A born entertainer, he knew how to engage the audience and make them laugh.

I enjoyed standing up on stage for the first time, in my *Gone with the Wind* romantic retro outfit, with jodhpurs, boots and billowing shirt sleeves. I felt self-assured with my look at that time. Mind you, I did get complaints going through immigration with my bearded bespectacled passport photo. Now I looked younger, for the first time in years I was being asked for my ID in American bars despite being twenty-six.

Despite our initial concerns, everything was opening up for the band at this time. My album *Voyage* was gaining a ton of interest in the States. The A&R guru for Chrysalis

Russ Shaw insisted I show up at as many radio stations as possible before each Genesis show. Shaker and mover Ahmet Ertegun, head of Atlantic now graced our New York show. He said "Hey, you guys are good! We're gonna get right behind you." I wondered if he'd be true to his word, but he was. Suddenly, whenever we arrived at each airport, two reps from Atlantic would meet us. We were getting huge publicity and were given priority treatment.

The *Trick* tour lasted about six months. I felt the pressure, and often it was a relief to hang out with the crew who were entertaining and relaxing company.

During the *Trick* tour we did five consecutive gigs at Hammersmith Odeon, which felt extraordinary. The band were on the up at this point. We were using a laser by then along with a heavyweight light show. Mike's use of the newly invented Taurus pedals particularly on 'Dance on a Volcano' was a stand-out feature. It could shake the foundations of any venue. A big bold brassy sound which opened up a whole new world of subsonics. I felt we were a force to be reckoned with and doors were opening continually. That combined with the success of *Acolyte* made a big difference for me.

Publicist Peter Thompson brought Mick Jagger to one of the Hammersmith shows. Mick was sufficiently impressed to say to Peter, "They'll probably be one of the biggest things around in a couple of years". It was a huge boost to our confidence, having as much of an impact in its way as the John Lennon comment had been three years earlier. Fantastic to draw plaudits from both a Beatle and a Rolling Stone.

I finally met Jagger a few years later in Brazil whilst he was making a video to promote his own solo work. "… 'Ere, Wot you doin' 'ere?", he asked. I explained I'd just been recording *Till We Have Faces* there. He appeared to be relieved to be speaking to a fellow Englishman in the midst of Brazilian mayhem with a huge invited crowd. He admitted that he was more than a little tired. It occurred to me that even the gods can become vulnerable. I felt he was like a ringmaster in the middle of his own circus... lions nearby, baying for blood and blues.

Some years on in the UK I encountered Mrs Jagger. Jerry Hall interviewed me on a cable TV show she hosted. There I was, hoping to present myself as a serious musician for technically demanding acoustic guitar work, when she shimmied up to the camera and whispered in conspiratorial tones, "And now we're gonna meet a genuine rock star..." "Oh no!" I thought, "Doesn't she have enough rock stars at home?" I half expected her to say, "I've never met a rock star before. What's it like?" She was wearing a very demure grey suit, but the tight skirt was pretty short, revealing those long Texan legs... Who would have guessed that she was to move on from Musos to Moguls, to reinvent herself as Mrs Rupert Murdoch.

As the *Trick* tour ended, I decided to rent my own place again. I moved out of my parents' home for the last time and rented a flat in Lawrence Street near the river in Chelsea from brilliant writer Nona Coxhead. Her passion was ESP and Biofeedback... many subjects relating to the power of the mind. She introduced me to Transcendental Meditation, which has always helped me since, acting as a conduit into the world of dreams, bringing much needed equilibrium at times of stress. It was good timing because sad news was just around the corner...

The summer was drawing to a close, and out of the blue one evening, Mum called. She was in tears, telling me she had split up with Dad. She was in a bad way and came over to stay with me that night. I was shocked because I hadn't seen it coming, but on reflection I realise they'd been leading separate lives for some time. They had fundamentally different needs. Apart from visits to the local pub, Dad preferred to stay at home and concentrate on his paintings, whilst Mum needed to be out as much as possible!

As the strong silent type, Dad spoke very little, but gregarious Mum would talk to virtually anybody about anything. She has always been intrigued by people, searching for the key to unlock them and to know what makes them tick. I can see now how she was more suited to her second husband Mike, who shares both her love of travel and socialising. I'm thrilled they have friends all over the globe.

But at the time, both Mum and Dad were devastated and when she turned up on my doorstep at night, she looked like she had only just survived a storm at sea. I'd never seen her look so vulnerable before. But she knew it was all over and never went back to Dad. I felt gutted for them both. I guess it happened at that time because both John and I had recently moved out of the family home and were fully launched. Now there was even less to hold Mum and Dad together. No-one was at fault. They'd just grown apart. They realised this as time went by and always remained friends.

My parents had always been a great support and had taken me in when I was at an all-time low during my first marriage break up. Now it was my turn to help them both. At different points over the following months they spent time with me. I was glad to help lift their spirits. The first time Dad stayed I cooked a meal for him and John. The three of us listened to Derek and Clive (Peter Cook and Dudley Moore) over several glasses and the laughter flowed with the wine. We were all boys together that night. Briefly that night the tragic time turned into a triumph for Dad as the walls shook with the sound of our combined laughter. I was so thrilled to see him happy. It was a small step on Dad's road to recovery. Within a few months he settled into another Pimlico flat near Ebury Bridge, where he happily continued to live and paint until 2007.

I briefly rented a couple of other apartments after Lawrence Street, but by the autumn of 1976 with the proceeds of *Voyage of the Acolyte* I was able to buy a property for the first time. It was a house in Princedale Road, Holland Park — a colourful part of town I'd always been drawn to. It was my first fully fledged home. Buying that little house was part of the growing up process. We think we're ready for everything at sixteen, but how little I knew at that age! Even ten years on in that eventful year, although my perception and judgements were often naive and misplaced, I was starting to leave behind the boy from Pimlico. Mum stayed for some months in my new house while she was finding her feet. For much of that time I was away on tour or recording.

This whole period was a defining one. Now that I'd let loose an album which had taken off in its own right, many creative ideas were flooding forth like a tsunami. I was ready to contribute songs and arrangements with complete confidence when we embarked on the *Wind and Wuthering* recordings. I felt I was no longer the new boy at the old school. It was an important distinction from my humble attitude of the earlier years.

Wind and Wuthering was recorded in early autumn 1976 in Relight Studios, Hilvarenbeek, Holland. Many of my ideas saw the light of day on the album. I felt 'Blood on the Rooftops' explored new territory as it was subtly different structurally with a long guitar introduction. I was starting to incorporate nylon guitar into the picture much more, which

I felt gave the band an added dimension: unusual for rock. Whilst Phil wrote the chorus, I wrote the verse picturing a man and his son avoiding reality through the world of television — as with people in Plato's *The Cave,* only being able to experience life through watching shadow puppets move around a cave wall.

I wrote the music that was to become my solo track 'Please Don't Touch'. The bass drum rhythm for this was used with 'Wot Gorilla?'. The two tunes were originally linked. '…In That Quiet Earth' was a rare combination of my top line, Mike's chords and Phil's 6/4 rhythm. I wrote the song in the middle of 'Eleventh Earl of Mar' and the stomp riff.

We were happily sparking off each other and painting the picture with ease at this time. Tony's ideas still tended to be prioritised at the committee stage because Mike generally backed him up, but the music was sounding good.

The future was starting to present itself. In the corner at Relight Studios I found a new keyboard called the optigan… Lo-fi heaven for the one fingered keyboard player! It was to spark many a future song in the strangest way imaginable, such as 'Sentimental Institution' on *Defector.*

We opened the *Wind & Wuthering* show at The Rainbow Theatre in London. It was Chester Thompson's first gig with us. He was a great asset to the band with his Zappa and Weather Report credentials. The buzz from the audience was electric.

The band was moving from strength to strength. On arrival in the States in 1977 we appeared on the Mike Douglas TV show, which was a huge coup, turning us overnight into nationwide favourites.

We played Madison Square Garden for the first time where the atmosphere from the enormous crowd was

Dad Peter
around 1947.

(Photos Hackett Family Archive)

Mum June.

John with
Myself,
1956.

Me with Mum in 1950.

Me
aged five.

Playing cowboys and Indians with John and our pals in Canada, 1957.

Me with John.

(Colin McLeod)

The third gig with Genesis at London's Lyceum, 24th January 1971.

(Armando Gallo)

With Gold Discs presented for Selling England By The Pound in 1975.
Back row: L-R: Mike, Peter & our manager Tony Smith.
Front row, L-R: Tony, myself and Phil.

Backstage in 1977 with Tony, Chester, Mike & Phil.

(Armando Gallo)

Wind and Wuthering tour, 1977.

(Armando Gallo)

Genesis playing onstage, 1977.

(Armando Gallo)

Recording for *Please Don't Touch* with
Ritchie Havens, 1977.

(Armando Gallo)

1977 tour.

(Armando Gallo)

At the Reading Festival, 1979.

(rmando Gallo)

Back at the Reading Festival, 1981.

(Alan Perry Concert Photography)

Exchanging guitar ideas with Mike.

(Armando Gallo)Armando Gallo

Myself with Nick Magnus in 1984.

With Steve Howe on the GTR tour, 1986.

Ben Castle, Phil Mulford, Roger King, Gary O'Toole and mysef whilst on tour in Italy, 2000.

(Roger Salem)

2010 tour.

(Lee Millward)

Nick Beggs, Anthony Phillips and Chris Squire with myself and Jo on our wedding day, 2011.

(Tish Dodd)

Genesis Revisited at the Royal Albert Hall, London, 2013.

Angela & Maurizio Vicedomini

Reunited with Phil, Tony, Peter and Mike, 2014.

(Jo Hackett)

In Machu Picchu.

(Jo Hackett)

With wolves in Italy.

(Jo Hackett)

Myself and Jo in the Meenakshi Temple, India.

Riding the camel at the pyramids, Egypt.

Jo Hackett

The band along with Amanda Lehmann and the Heart Of England orchestra conducted by Bradley Thachuk, 2018.

(photo by Lee Millward)

With John Wetton at the Royal Albert Hall, 2013.

(photo by Angela Vicedomini)

With Bruce Willis backstage in New York, 2015.

(Jo Hackett)

US 2018 tour.

(Rick Pauline)

Genesis Revisited show – Hammersmith Apollo, London, 2019.

(Lee Millwa...

(Jo Hack...

Nad, Jonas, myself, Rob, Craig and Roger backstage, 2019.

Hackett tour team UK 2019.

extraordinary. They were on their feet from the first note of 'Squonk'. It was as if Genesismania had arrived…

But increased success wasn't without complication. The union had to be bribed to allow us to put the show on. This wasn't the first time we'd had those kinds of problems. An earlier show in New York had to be cancelled on *The Lamb Lies Down on Broadway* tour when equipment was stolen from the venue. When a ransom was paid, we got the equipment back and we were able to reschedule. All part and parcel of the New York experience.

Back to 1977, when we played the LA Forum a strange sound started to emanate from the drums while Phil was singing. It turned out to be a kid who'd managed to get up on stage and get himself behind the drum kit! Unfortunately, the security guys didn't just remove the kid from the stage but beat him up badly, which to my mind was brutal and unnecessary. But unaware at that moment, the band played on.

Whilst I was in LA, I met up with head of A&R at Chrysalis Russ Shaw, who'd been a big part of making *Voyage* a success in the States. Russ was a friend of Rod Stewart. On his wall was a beach photo of him with Rod running around in their Bermuda shorts. He pointed out a huge billboard which constantly advertised Rod on Sunset Boulevard. Russ invited me to have dinner at the famous Dome restaurant. We'd just arrived as Rod suddenly appeared with a bunch of pals and starlets. We all went back to Rod's palatial art nouveau-style home. Everyone watched with reverence and delight, having a Rodtastic time, as dressed in white Rod danced around on his own in his private disco. I was amused and felt happily off the hook until one guy suddenly lurched towards me, grabbed hold of my shoulders and tried to kiss me, at which point I decided it was time to leave and

I hightailed it out of the place… beating a hasty retreat until I reached the safety of my hotel.

The LA scene was a strange one indeed. I remember meeting sweet, talkative songwriter Jackie de Shannon at a plush Hollywood party laid on for Genesis, where she told me we must be doing well as they wouldn't bother to put on a glitzy party for us in LA otherwise.

LA had a disingenuous side. In local shops they wanted to know who you were and if therefore you were anyone remotely important. You could smell the impermanence, as fleeting as a whiff of perfume. Shop fronts came and went like constantly changing movie scenery. Friendships were made instantly but few lasted. They either loved you or ignored you… nothing in between.

I didn't want to be a permanent fixture, but despite the fake aspect, Tinseltown was a thrilling place to visit. I enjoyed the constant heat of endless summer and loved quirky places like the Hi Pockets restaurant in Santa Monica where waiters and waitresses would suddenly burst into song between taking orders. Surf City had a theatrical air. Santa Monica Pier also held a fascination. Its malevolent merry-go-round with those horse heads coming at you was featured in *The Sting*, and I was to use sounds from its arcade on my *Please Don't Touch* album.

In Genesis we'd scored in LA from the word go, having sold out the Roxy for three nights running even on the first visit. By 1977 around 20,000 people were filling LA venues, with people queuing overnight before showtime. LA took us to its heart first, whilst a ripple effect then spread out to the rest of the States.

When Genesis returned to the UK to play three nights in London at Earls Court, sales went like wildfire and the show was broadcast live on Capital Radio, giving the band a huge plug at home. Although I was to leave the band shortly after to pursue my own path, I'm still proud of those gigs.

Richie Havens supported us on all three nights. I went backstage to meet him and told him how much I admired his incredible singing. I'd never forgotten hearing that super-human voice which rode the storm as thunder and lightning raged above the 1970 Isle of Wight Festival. He sounded like a god to me, and after the last Earls Court night suddenly, this deity was coming to dinner at my new little house. Mum cooked a great meal, whilst Richie offered to help wash the dishes. It felt as if we'd always known each other. I think that gave Mum a boost too during her difficult road to recovery after splitting up with Dad. I was dying all evening to pop the question of whether Richie would work with me or not, but I didn't want to be too pushy. Luckily for me he suggested it, and I knew then that he would be a huge plus if his presence graced my next solo album.

During that summer of 1977 when I took up Transcendental Meditation, in the middle of a meditation I heard Richie Havens singing and I immediately felt uplifted by the song's melody and words arriving in one go, a transcendent moment like no other... I phoned him instantly and told him what I had in mind. He said he could hear it already and that it sounded great!

By this time, I was nothing like the apologetic newcomer who'd joined Genesis. My confidence had grown a great deal over the years with musical experience and on the road. And now I already had a successful solo album under my belt. It also helped that the band was by this time becoming a world force, a collection of songwriters to rival the best in our field.

When Pete left in 1975 it shook us to the core and

we were concerned about our future as a band, but once Phil was promoted to front man it became clear that we were going places.

I really loved making my first album *Voyage of the Acolyte,* but at that time I hoped to balance solo projects whilst staying in Genesis. In fact, both Mike and Phil were supportive when I was making the album and worked with me on some of the material. Tony Smith was also helpful and encouraging. As soon as I'd finished recording *Voyage* I was back with the Genesis guys rehearsing and recording *A Trick of the Tail.* The vibe was good and we had a ton of innovative ideas for the album.

Events were taking off in a huge way when we toured *A Trick of the Tail* in 1976. We were playing in front of much larger audiences than before and carried a heavyweight light show. This combined with the success of my solo album was a heady combination. At times I could feel my fingers fly across the strings and the guitar sounded stronger than ever. I was also thrilled that Phil had developed into a real lead singer. Fans took to him, his voice sounded amazing and he had great stage presence in his dual role of drummer and front man.

My concerns regarding the band situation began on one occasion during the 1976 tour. Chrysalis (the US record company) was giving me some attention as *Voyage of the Acolyte* had just come out on their label and was doing well. But although the band had agreed to me being filmed in one soundcheck for album promotion, Mike threw down his bass in annoyance. Later that day he and Tony asked me to meet them on my own and informed me that they didn't want me to do any more solo projects whilst remaining a member of the band. I was taken aback as Mike had been pro the recording of *Voyage* and had worked on it with me. Although I was worried about this change of attitude within the band, things were going so well for us all that I didn't make a fuss. Plus, I hoped that they would again be supportive once time had passed.

I enjoyed our time of recording *Wind & Wuthering* and to this day I'm proud of that album. There were some disputes over credits which concerned me, but I knew we all pulled off something special. The band continued to go from strength to strength on the tour, playing stunningly to even larger crowds than before.

It was off the road that the problem once again surfaced. My decision to leave the band solidified when we were mixing *Seconds Out,* mixing the same music we'd been touring for many months. Chrysalis was keen for me to deliver another solo album and by now it was two years since the recording of *Voyage.* By this time, I was brimming over with musical ideas, some of which had already been rejected by the band, and I knew it was time to complete another solo project.

Again, I met resistance to doing another album of my own whilst continuing to be a part of the band. If they had been relaxed about my moving between the band and solo projects, it would have been fine. Leaving the band was a very hard decision to make, particularly given everything we had been through and achieved together, but I realised my need for autonomy was becoming stronger than the benefits of staying with the team.

In recent times, Tony said in an interview for *Prog* magazine that he missed me after I left and that he felt some of the songs on the following album would have been stronger if I'd stayed. I appreciated that comment, which showed reflection and consideration on his part. We've all maintained friendship over the years, and there is mutual respect. I saw the show Genesis put on following *Duke* and I was impressed. I could see what audiences had always loved about Genesis, with that distinctive sound, great talent and fab light show.

But back in 1977 I needed to be strong to follow through with my decision. The day I left was unplanned. I suddenly realised I had to leave. I felt terrible and initially I wondered if I had done the right thing. In retrospect, I can see that perhaps I could have eventually found a way through. Phil worked on and off already at that time with Brand X and indeed the Genesis guys have all had solo projects over the years, including Phil's solo career as well as Mike's Mike and the Mechanics whilst maintaining the band. But I don't have any regrets and I'm extremely proud of the solo work I've done and continue to create to this day. There would only have been time for some of that music to gestate and surface if I'd stayed with the group. Ultimately, I'm able to express myself most fully as solo artist. The truth is that even though I would've stayed longer if there had been more flexibility, I don't regret leaving Genesis. It was great to be a part of that incredible team, but I had to answer my inner muse. It was time to move on. An extraordinary creative door had opened for me when I joined the group, and now I found myself walking through another one nearly seven years down the line. It was a calling. Once again, I was up on that wall, and I made the decision to take another leap of faith into the abyss.

7

Through screaming tunnels the engine sings...

The day after I left the band, I had lunch with Mum and John. They were supportive and understanding although like me, they were nervous about whether I'd made the right decision. I knew there was no other path I could follow in all conscience, but I remember lying in bed on my own night after night worrying. Had I done the right thing? It was a big risk and a huge step into the unknown. I was leaving a world class band that was by now filling arenas internationally. I had to trust in the power of my instinct and inspiration. I knew I needed to remain as strong and confident as possible, knowing music is its own reward and holds its own currency.

When I left Genesis, I already had many ideas that I knew would not have worked with the band. I needed to spread my wings. When an idea is that strong you realise it has to be born. Ideas not developed have always felt to me like unborn children. I realised it was going to be a long hard slog, but I felt it best to take action and get down to the album I'd wanted to do for so long as fast as possible.

I immediately set about preparing for the album. I bought a Roland GR 500 guitar synth, which sounded like a cross between brass and a harmonium. The important thing was that it sounded nothing like a guitar. I could make unusual sounds with it. It formed the basis of the sound on 'Land of a Thousand Autumns'. When it sustained it stared you right between the eyes. Its noise was like a fiery oriental dragon waking from slumber, plus I wanted to give the mythical beast its own voice, via a minor scale with Far Eastern promise.

At home I sang demos of the vocals. I also made my voice into voice loops so we could have 24 notes on a mixing console, all singing Aahh. This made up those voices on 'The Voice of Necam'.

I chose to record in LA because I wanted to interact with Chrysalis as much as possible to make some impact on America as well as Europe. Singers and musicians were lined up who lived over there too, including outstanding singer Steve Walsh. I loved his voice on Kansas' 'Carry on My Wayward Son'. Both US based Richie Havens and Randy Crawford had agreed to sing on the album too. I wanted a hybrid between black soul and white rock music, working with people who were great improvisers.

In her own inimitable style, Randy Crawford did a terrific job on 'Hoping Love Will Last'. This track was linked to my sadness about the end of my parents' relationship, but also personal feelings, which influenced 'Icarus Ascending' too. But the music took on a transcendent life of its own, opening up into whole new continents of possibility.

I was entranced by Richie Havens' voice and his extraordinarily positive outlook. Working with him was absolutely thrilling. He could sing anything and make it sound like he'd been doing it all his life. Every word sounded believable from his mouth. He was a giant among singers. He let rip with the outro of 'Icarus Ascending' which I felt was like the final flight of the phoenix. I continued to be a fan of his god-like voice.

Many years later I saw him at the Jazz Café in London performing a field holler face down into the floor, getting louder and louder, raising the energy to enormous proportions. It reminded me of the magic moment at the Isle of Wight Festival in 1970 when his voice powered through the thunderstorm at night as if he was the voice of the storm, with thunder and lightning as his percussion effects. All of us in Genesis had been taken by his unique voice, whilst Phil and I also loved his fast strumming guitar style.

Exploring potential Californian studios, I found a fantastic pipe organ in the Record Plant, which I used on 'Icarus Ascending' and the flagship tune 'Please Don't Touch'. For the title track we went all out to make that huge sound.

I've often found that neither weather nor time interfaced with recording. A studio becomes what John Acock referred to as "The Timeless Void". You're not aware of how much time has passed by. I've always thrown myself so much into a body of work that I need recovery time after it. Recording *Please Don't Touch*, I also suffered a ton of stress working with so many people and teams who all had different ways of doing things. But musical magic was captured by Armando Gallo's beautiful photos.

Recording in the States was thrilling but heavily intensive, timewise and emotionally. On my return to the UK I fell ill with stomach ulcers and was admitted to hospital on Christmas Eve. I needed a break.

As the new year of 1978 arrived, I was out of hospital and over the course of the winter I finished shaping the album. Whenever I recorded abroad, I always felt the need to rationalise it back in England where I could complete it with a final sense of identity. The effect of being away from home creates an exotic, dreamlike atmosphere, but I've always felt more grounded back on home turf.

There was great response to *Please Don't Touch*. Many years later Steven Wilson told me that it was his *Sergeant Pepper* when he was exposed to it at eleven years old. I was thrilled with my hard fought for album, but I didn't yet have the confidence to go out on tour and front my own band. In fact, the prospect was terrifying! However, Ian Wright of MAM Agency convinced me I should bite the bullet. He knew my name would carry enough weight to fill halls in Europe and Scandinavia, and Wright was right... He became my manager and we set about putting a band together.

John with his beautiful flute playing was an obvious choice. He was also a fluent guitarist and had a way of playing the bass pedals raised on a stand, hammering them with his fists. With his young, handsome looks, his nickname amongst the band was Teen Idol. Many a maiden swooned to the silver notes of his flute and the thrilling vibrations of those bass pedals...

When I called up Nick Magnus, he initially thought it was a prank call, because a mate of his had just been the victim of a hoax call from an apparent Keith Emerson! Luckily, I convinced Nick that it was me and I think he was relieved to see me turn up at his front door. He was really impressive. At one point I said I wished I had a pipe organ sound, to which he replied, "It just happens that I have it!" He then made the sound of a glorious cathedral organ on full throttle. His secret weapon was a personally modified Vox String Thing. Nick gained my mighty Mellotron, whilst I gained a 'pipe organ' along with a fantastic keyboard player and future collaborator. Later on-stage he often used to dress like an American motorcycle cop, complete with handcuffs dangling from his belt, and American audience members often used to ask if he was a real cop!

I remember John Sheerer turning up with his massive gleaming oil rig of a drum kit. He was a powerful player with an extraordinary degree of self-confidence. It became increasingly apparent that he was a born showman. He'd turn up at rehearsals in a Rolls Royce and fur coat. On stage he'd often be stripped to the waist, wearing the tightest pair of spandex trousers imaginable. When introduced, he'd stand on his drum stool, wiggling his bum at the crowd to cat calls, wolf whistles and loud applause.

Tall, handsome Dik Cadbury was clearly a very accurate bass player from the start, with a great singing voice, having also been trained as a counter tenor. He was to become the go-to man to arrange vocal harmonies.

From the moment I heard Pete Hicks' voice, I felt it had a beautiful velvety quality. He was fabulous as lead singer, but I also realised we had this gorgeous vocal harmony sound. Pete's humour often had us in stitches. On some versions of *Spectral Mornings* you can hear him doing an impression of a grumpy caretaker, having to clear up the mess left behind by spoiled rock stars he wouldn't even pay with shirt buttons.

With this crack regiment, I embarked on my first solo tour in the autumn of 1978, playing numbers from *Voyage* and *Please Don't Touch*, plus test driving one or two things that were to show up on *Spectral Mornings*. To say I was nervous for the first gig in Oslo is an understatement. I was running around backstage like a cat on a hot tin roof! Usually I have a calm facade, but have been known to lose it when I'm anxious.

Despite concerns, the show went off like a rocket, and the tour sold out. Full of nervous energy, excitement swiftly bit through the chains of fear. It was fabulous to bring all that music to life at shows and the band were brilliant. We had some great characters on that tour, such as our Welsh bus driver, "Will the Bus", a larger than life personality with a propensity to drive undaunted the wrong way up streets to speed things along... In Monaco when confronted with a French speaking gendarme, W the B just smiled and said, "Do you speak Welsh boyo…?"

I came to love the band and we had a ball on the road. I was on a huge high from that first tour, and so was everyone else. We couldn't wait to get started on an album together. I was confident we could all make a tremendously varied amount of music and a great album. For the first time in my life I'd arrived as a solo act with a proud band of quirky and gifted personalities.

From recording on the sunny shores of California for *Please Don't Touch*, to a ghostly frozen winter wonderland lake in Holland for *Spectral Mornings* in January '79, *Spectral* was to have a different atmosphere. Whilst *Please Don't Touch* had an eclectic Anglo-American sound, *Spectral* had more of a theme with a sense of a journey and spiritual thread, more like *Acolyte*.

I'm not religious, but from tarot cards to spiritual dimensions, I've always explored the paranormal and life beyond life... I don't buy either the Heaven and Hell idea or reincarnation as I believe both concepts were designed to keep people in their places… But to this day I feel there is some kind of existence after death.

By 1979 I was inspired by visits I'd recently made to the Spiritualist Association of Great Britain. Their library was full of intriguing books, and one medium recounted names of several people I knew with an amazing insight into their characters. I had another experience later on with a cab driver, who claimed to have had the gift of mediumship since being resuscitated after a car accident. Not only did he recount correct names, but he predicted an imminent unexpected death in the family, which occurred a week later when my grandfather suddenly died, having had robust health up to that point.

The cab driver encounter was freaky, and I think I would have preferred not to have had that piece of information, but it followed a pattern. People I've known over the years have had experiences of connecting with departed loved ones, and I have too. There seems to be a link or thread.

In a more general sense, the passing of a life or way of life and the beginning of the new within a lifetime also inspired me... the whole idea of doors closing and opening throughout our lives. I always sensed the constant cycle of death and rebirth going on throughout life. My recent departure from Genesis sparked off many questions, bubbling up to the surface and inspiring the framework that formed *Spectral Mornings*.

The album was recorded in Hilversum, Holland, where temperatures had plummeted way below freezing. Locals had reckless fun performing handbreak turns in their cars, pirouetting perilously in a frenzied heavy metal ballet, driving like there was no tomorrow... Ice Road Truckers looks like a doddle by comparison!

The huge studio was its own protective bubble. Whilst the snow queen worked her mischief outside, inside was warm and inviting. Food and drink were constantly on tap. The studio janitor and night watchman Freek enjoyed the music so much, he cheered us on and opened the drinks cabinet so we could help ourselves to anything we wanted. Fuelled by the scotch and coke from that famous cabinet along with regular doses of weed in a land where it was legal and even encouraged, we were on a high. As a band of pals we worked and played hard and partied 'til we dropped.

'Spectral Mornings' was the first track recorded. Nick Magnus' keyboards, like a pipe organ on full stun, gave the track that huge sound along with the guitar. We knew immediately we were on to a winner. There was a sense of a departed spirit flying free on this song.

'Tigermoth' was more overtly linked to the afterlife, with its story of a sympathetic spirit helping a discarnate airman who doesn't realise he's dead after being shot down in an air battle. Nick created the aerial dogfight cleverly on the synth, along with John's spiralling flute and Dik's bass pedals sounding like the drone of a Lancaster bomber.

By contrast, I loved the koto which created the beautiful delicate sound on 'The Red Flower of Tai Chi Blooms Everywhere'. I've always enjoyed extreme contrasts between tracks on albums. 'Red Flower' also heralded a life-long interest in the sounds of far flung places, from China to India, South America to the Middle East and global influences… The less familiar, the more magical and intriguing.

I was particularly proud of 'Every Day'. Nick's various keyboards combined with my textures sounded like a third instrument, part pipe organ, part guitar… an immediately engaging sound. I used the Mellotron to reproduce loops of my voice. I went at the guitar with great joy on that track. It felt like a huge release of pent up frustrations, plus a way of turning the sadness I'd felt for years about my first girlfriend's drug addiction and the gulf that came between us into a triumphant theme. It was a song to blow away cobwebs, a breath of fresh air. I knew we were producing something powerful.

On this album the theme of endings and beginnings continued with 'The Virgin and the Gypsy', which came together when we doubled the 12-string parts with two harpsichords. John then played a couple of beautiful spontaneous flute solos sounding like two young lovers wrapping themselves around each other, whilst Pete Hicks sang a lovely vocal on his own. Doing the chorus in octaves gave it that extra polish and beautiful sound. My idea of answering harmonies was beautifully orchestrated by Dik Cadbury. It was a magical number held together by slender threads. Sensual in nature, it was a song of the earth involving two characters who couldn't refuse each other, breaking down an old-world order.

My new world order was now thriving. Things had come a long way in a time of growing certainty. in the eighteen months since leaving Genesis. Like *Acolyte, Spectral* turned out to be a chart success.

On the downside, I wasn't being entirely responsible. Smoking dope and drinking most nights during recording, I was still sailing close to the wind despite being hospitalised after recording the previous album!

By the time I returned home I was sick again. I was a pitiful state. I had to check mixes from my couch and sometimes even the bed because I was too sick to get to the studio, struggling on my own in the house. So, why did I make myself ill again? The pressure to build on *Acolyte* and *Please Don't Touch* was hard to handle, despite growing success and great band achievements. Since childhood with so many put downs at school, I'd never been a naturally confident person. I needed to see and feel success at each stage... Life felt suspended on a knife edge in those days, obsessing with every note, still feeling I had something to prove.

And then there was a sell-out tour. Crowds were fantastic. They raised the roof at every venue. Along with the excitement, everything went like clockwork but there were some hairy moments. My flame haired Irish guitar tech Ged had a reputation for being quick with his fists. At one venue, he even knocked out the promotor, assuming he was a fan trespassing on the stage. Gigs could be pretty wild in those days.

Charisma chose the ICA Arts Centre, a great venue for the launch of *Spectral Mornings*. Anne Nightingale presented it and Alan Freeman (Fluff) attended. Since I was a kid I'd enjoyed listening to his shows, and now he'd become a friend and avid supporter. The reaction to the album was terrific and it charted for over three months. The *Spectral* tour riding on the back of the album, drew huge audiences. We'd come into our own. I was so proud of the band.

Dependency on Genesis had finally turned into an ancient dream from a previous life. The fears that had plagued me ever since my departure from the big machine had receded into a distant dark corner. My dreams, welling up from subconscious images, had reached the surface and were now being celebrated.

This 'circus of becoming' had finally arrived and hit its zenith at the Reading Festival of August '79. Once the band kicked off it was incredibly loud on stage and off. As 'Please Don't Touch' thundered over the crowd, it had never sounded so powerful. I felt we were in the eye of the storm. The circus hit town and demolished all in its path. But as we often find, the triumphal moment is often followed by the appearance of a dark cloud on the horizon…

By the summer of 1979 I was thrilled by the initial wave of success. Creative inspiration seemed limitless. However, the first of several new combative challenges was already starting to raise its head.

Spectral Mornings had been proudly up there in the charts and gigs were selling out, but reviews were often abysmal. A typical example read, "I'm surprised that people still listen to this kind of rubbish anymore." Where was this coming from? The answer is clear. A new batch of aliens had landed and were taking over.

Punk had arrived.

I realised the new order was there in force when to get into a record shop in King's Road one day I had to push through a clump of spiky green and puke haired, spotty, sneering punks bedecked in safety pins and razors.

Initially I thought it was a joke. I remember buying the Sex Pistols' first record, which raised a smile and fitted nicely with my *Derek and Clive* collection. But once Punk effectively took up arms against every other genre of music, the press jumped on the bandwagon and hostility became the norm. With Punk leading the charge, ignorance was now hailed as virtue. I heard its proponents say, "You don't need skill, who needs standards? Any crap will do if you sling enough of it at the walls." It wasn't so much a case of a new broom which swept clean, as a bristling loo brush that infected all in its path. Now every other style was under attack for being too romantic, fussy or pretentious. Marketing had triumphed over content and nihilism held sway.

A sinister form of dictatorship took hold. Journalists were losing their jobs if they refused to follow the party line. *Melody Maker*, the very paper which had put me in touch with the Genesis guys, like many other music papers that were prevalent in the seventies, eventually went out of business. Many musicians' careers were effectively destroyed. Music itself was in the dock. Those of us who survived the Punk tsunami had to be increasingly tenacious. Many chose to become more musically superficial and accessible. Some, such as Pink Floyd with *The Wall* managed to bridge the gap, maintaining their musical style, whilst aligning themselves to an anti-establishment concept aimed at the walking wounded. I took a similar path with my next album.

I continued to follow an eclectic musical road, but the subject matter was less romantic and more grounded, with a hint of rebellion. It frustrated me to be viewed as an establishment figure, when that was what I'd always fought against. Constructive rebellion was my calling card. My long hair had been a flash point in the 1960s, the ad in *Melody Maker* had challenged the limitations of music, and on leaving Genesis I'd torn up the rule book of corporate rock, steering my own creative wheelbarrow through a landscape of unlikely styles. The title *Defector* suited me personally, as I'd already set myself up as a separate and free entity. It also reflected the material on the album.

I aimed to do something earthy. *Spectral Mornings* had dealt with survival of the spirit after death. Now I was dealing with a different kind of survival. The world was becoming increasingly politically unstable at the time. Extremists had taken over in Iran whilst storming of the American embassy and hostage taking was their calling card. Sabre rattling between East and West dominated the news... My awareness that Soviet Communism would collapse from within (as it did ten years later) inspired the concept of *Defector*.

I saw a parallel between people escaping from the Eastern Bloc and myself as a defector from the well-oiled machine of Genesis... Of course, Genesis wasn't a sinister organisation, but the subtext was still the need for freedom from something constraining and you can't keep a good man down.

The song 'Leaving' had the sleepwalking feel of a drugged dissident who was being exchanged. I was imagining the problem of the Western media questioning this man, insensitive to what he had just been through. I was influenced by Aleksandr Solzhenitsyn's *One Day in the Life of Ivan Denisovich* which depicted the worst horrors of the Soviet Union. I also reflected on the way excessive importance is attached to sensation, celebrity and materialism in the West. I could see the other side of the coin here, as with my own situation. I was relieved to be a solo act, but it had its downside. I felt under pressure, caught in the crossfire of record companies in corporate reshuffles. With people constantly being replaced it was hard to build up a working relationship in a troubled and jaded business.

Much of the colouring of 'Leaving' came from Nick Magnus' keyboards with his clever use of vocoder and synth, impersonating an Ondes Martinot. Nick arranged 'Hammer in the Sand' too. When I heard him trying out the melody on keyboards, I knew he'd created the best version of it.

'Slogans' was in keeping with the gritty aspect of the album. Nick used a vocoder which gave an electronic sound to the words blah, blah, blah... Highlighting meaningless propaganda, whilst the whole track hurtled along like an angry war machine.

We created the reverb drum sound for 'The Steppes' in an echoing church, giving it the weight it needed. From the 'The Steppes' to 'Sentimental Institution', the tracks ranged from sombre to light-hearted. As with most of my albums, I didn't stick rigidly to a theme, because I prefer my musical pictures to be coloured at the edges.

We worked on *Defector* at Wessex Studios in London, where several acts were recording at the same time, including Chrissie Hynde and The Pretenders. Talented, but competitive when playing games between takes, Chrissie was happy when she beat me at pool, but furious when Nick Magnus beat her at Space Invaders…

Despite *Defector's* top ten chart success and the relatively socially oriented approach, I still was being hung, drawn and quartered by a Punk influenced press in the UK. The time of struggles was far from over. The USA was now embracing an MTV dominated scene. Chrysalis had recently taken on Blondie and was moving towards a more pop and singles-oriented market, so passed on *Defector* and I had to find another company out there. It was becoming more difficult to get albums released in the States. To be a new face on the block was all important. Marketing triumphed over content on both sides of the Pond. I knew I had the goods musically, but corporate America was turning a deaf ear to musicians and fans alike. Even Peter Gabriel changed record companies at that time in the States because the guys at Atlantic didn't appreciate his hugely influential third album. Musos and fans got it, but companies didn't.

After reading a particularly unpleasant article in the *NME* about me, I was pleased to receive a standing ovation at the De Montfort Hall, Leicester, home of *Genesis Live*. It was a validation of my personal efforts in the face of press hostility. Touring *Defector* broke box office records internationally and I was glad I'd stuck to my guns through all the flak.

We had several high points, including the day Phil Collins came to see the show at the Roxy, LA. He praised Pete Hicks' singing and said he enjoyed the show. The tour went like a dream, except for one point in Sittard, Netherlands, where the crew weren't given enough time to set up and my precious vintage Gibson Les Paul was knocked off its stand. The machine head was sheered off, but roadie Ged glued it back on. He did a fantastic job, as that is how it's been ever since, and I still enjoy playing that magic box to this day.

Although everything had gone so well, a new problem was rearing its head... It was becoming financially impossible to keep the band on a full-time retainer, whilst band members were also getting a tad restless, understandably wanting to have a stronger hand in the writing. I was sympathetic, but I'd given up Genesis to run a solo career and I didn't want to feel compromised. Much as I loved them, I realised a change was in the air. They clearly felt a need to spread their own wings as well.

A new chapter was opening... I planned to move forward with Nick Magnus, my brother John, and John Acock. As I write this, I'm nostalgic for John Acock, who died not so long ago. Not only was he an incredibly talented engineer, but he was also one of the nicest guys you'd ever want to meet, with a great sense of humour. He always looked young, even the last time I saw him at his 60th birthday. I'll remember sweet, gentle John forever with great affection.

Worthy of note is John's sense of humour with his fun stories. My favourite was his brief encounter with Vangelis (of *Chariots of Fire* fame). Delivering tapes to the Greek God of the keyboards one day, John knocked on his door. A voice boomed out, "Come in, John!" As John walked in, he saw Vangelis reclining on a chaise Longue, dressed in a one piece leopard skin leotard, whilst being fed grapes one at a time from a large bunch held above his head by a young dusky maiden...

Having let go of the band and aware of the constant hammering I was still receiving from the UK press whilst being increasingly marginalised by USA record company problems, I knew I had to think hard about the best course of action. I decided to bridge the gulf by making a simpler, more accessible album than usual. I couldn't sustain live shows without selling records to fund them. I was in a total Catch 22 situation. I also chose to take on lead vocals, no longer so dependent on others. In the main, I worked on the album just with Nick Magnus, brother John and John Acock. Much of it had a more poppy sound than before, but I did sometimes let rip, as with 'Air Conditioned Nightmare', which I'm still proud of.

At Redan Studios, Queensway, on Nick's suggestion we used a lift shaft with a speaker at the top and mic at the bottom to create the gated explosive drum sound. 'Overnight Sleeper' was inspired by a dream that coincidentally both Nick and I had of being trapped, dodging trains on railway lines between steep banks... The imagination was still running, and I couldn't resist adding in my acoustic piece, 'Cradle of Swans', the title of which was dream inspired.

This album was named *Cured* because I'd generally ended up sick with exhaustion at the end of albums and tours and now, short of checking into the Betty Ford clinic, I decided to clean up my act. I drew the line at eating Brussels Sprouts (can't even stand to be in the same house with them) but I took up running and swimming in a bid to improve health... I attempted to give up the poisons, but as you can see by my dozy expression on the cover of *Cured*, I was tucking into a Piña Colada (my second) and I still enjoyed the occasional joint. Frankly, the title gives a false impression.

On the day *Cured* was released on 14th August 1981 I married Kim at Chelsea Town Hall, London. My *Cured* tour began soon after.

The tour went smoothly, except for a couple of incidents... On one occasion lights caught fire on the stage of the Old Waldorf in San Francisco. At the same venue, all audience attention suddenly went to stage right and some girls from the crowd started to scream. The huge PA stack on that side was rocking backwards and forwards, in danger of tumbling down into the crowd. It transpired that one of the road crew was at it with a young lady up against the back of the stack! The same guy who shall remain nameless also had a penchant for taking all his clothes off and wandering up and down the aisles on transatlantic flights and was sometimes spotted stark naked, seated at the side of the stage with a box on his head.

For the *Cured* tour I had a new rhythm section, featuring Chas Cronk on bass and Ian Mosley on drums. Chas was a strong player who doubled me on vocals. A very sweet guy, who's now worked with Strawbs for many years. Ian was explosive on drums, usually taking the tempos at a new fast pace. He was to create a fantastic speedy 7/8 on *Highly Strung*'s 'Always Somewhere Else', originally recorded in a metal lined drum room. He had a brilliant sense of humour, describing his previous solo career as a milkman in tour brochures, and purposely creating terrible sounds on pianos to make us all laugh. For many years subsequently, he has toured with the phenomenally successful Marillion, alongside other pals, Steve Rothery, Pete Trewavas, Steve Hogarth, Mark Kelly and original singer Fish.

Fish is a fantastic larger than life character, always raising a smile. Today my wife Jo and I remain pals with Ian along with his wife / Marillion manager Lucy. Steve Rothery and his wife Jo are also great friends of ours. Steve and I enjoy playing together as well, and we've recently recorded some currently unreleased material.

My energy was low after *Cured*. I felt the need to find a way back to my vital centre. A doctor friend suggested I needed to go on holiday and do everything on offer and get involved in as many things as possible. It reminded me of a quote I read in D H Lawrence's *The Virgin and the Gypsy*, to be "braver in the body"... to find a conduit back to the musically adventurous spirit I am naturally. I'd become a competent gymnast many years earlier at school, and now I decided to push my physical boundaries once again.

On holiday to Bermuda I aimed to try whatever I could. The first experience of scuba diving was amazing, particularly standing on the ocean floor looking at the sunlight penetrating through the water. Encountering sea life first hand was totally uplifting, swimming through shoals of fish whilst floating through underwater gardens. Unfortunately, on my third undersea adventure I accidentally disconnected from my air supply. Holding my breath, I panicked. Was this it? We had a 'buddy system' but through the murky depths, I couldn't see anyone. Subaquatic sand was swirling around me. The seconds were ticking, the pressure of water was increasing in my ears and I felt I was about to lose consciousness. Luckily at the last minute one member of the group approached and realising I was in distress, reattached my air supply. I started to breathe normally but decided to head for the surface, slowly to avoid the bends. Once on dry land I realised my ears were still blocked. Terrified of potential deafness, I felt I'd had a warning and I never repeated the experience.

My next big adventure was water skiing. I was spectacularly unsuccessful at this. I stood on the skis at the ready anticipating an exciting flight, skimming the waves, but as soon as the boat took off, I sank and was dragged under water at a fast rate of knots with my feet in front of me. I couldn't coordinate the act of standing up and it was terrifying to once again be trapped in a situation where I couldn't breathe below the ocean surface... I had to let go of the rope and swim as fast as possible with skis on my feet to get my head above water. After three attempts, high speed drowning was taking its toll and I wisely gave up!

From water to snow... Then came my one and only great skiing expedition at Lake Tahoe in California. I thought I was doing quite well, speeding down the mountain on a high, watching the world race by, until suddenly to my horror I found I couldn't stop. Ahead of me down below appeared a bunch of about thirty tiny school kids, and I was heading at a terrifying pace towards them in a direct line. I was obviously about to die, possibly taking thirty little skittles with me... Disaster was just seconds away and there was nothing I could do. Out of desperation I wrapped my arm around a pole, wrenching my shoulder, but amazingly I didn't dislocate it and no kids were harmed. Needless-to-say, I decided there and then that speedy manoeuvres had better remain on the fretboard rather than on the slopes of doom.

But still game to try anything new, in Brazil I accepted an offer to try hang gliding off the top of a mountain. It was a double kite that enabled two people to fly. The idea of jumping off a mountain seemed great until the moment I had to take the plunge and run into potential oblivion. I believe the rush of adrenaline was so great, I momentarily passed out. It was literally a heart stopping moment. I confess I felt pure fear. Lying in the harness that looks like a large duffle bag attached by a piece of string to a flimsy cloth sail, it was disconcerting to look down. Although the view was magnificent, I never for one moment lost my fear. The warm air spiralled us up even higher than the mountain. We flew for forty minutes, every now and again plummeting downwards whenever I reached out for the bar, instinctively wanting something to hold on to. When we finally hit the ground running, I was still shaking. I believe this was the most foolhardy thing I ever did. Even many hang gliding 'experts' have lost their lives at the mercy of unpredictable air currents.

Whilst I was busy risking my life in Brazil, out of the blue I received a call from my Dad who said, "I've heard that your band mates are reforming with Peter Gabriel to do a show at Milton Keynes..." This was for a concert to enable Peter Gabriel to help out WOMAD, an organisation giving a chance to great musicians from around the world. Dad and I agreed that I should be a part of it.

The following day I hightailed it back to the UK and flew in to join the guys for the show. As they'd already rehearsed up their stuff, I was only able to join the encores, but I was thrilled to be involved with the team once more... Despite the heavens opening to incessant rain, the crowd was as enthusiastic as the band. Both on stage and backstage, we were all excited to make a rousing noise together again. It was a terrific atmosphere as we'd all come together for the right reasons... No profit motive... This was a move to help others out. We were hugging each other. The date coincided with Mike's birthday. Celebrations were in full swing, so the backstage party went on into the early hours... Pete broke into 'Auld Lang Syne' as we all linked arms. No stiff upper lips that night!

The Milton Keynes get together made me feel that anything was possible...

At this time I had a series of extraordinary dreams about a rectangular glass pavilion. On each visit, there was a new message. The first time, the building was empty but I sensed the presence of spirits. I heard a voice which said, "If you want to connect with them, let the spirits get a good look at you first."

Coincidentally, in my waking life I'd just discovered the power of spiritual healing. A healer had worked on my painful foot which had bothered me for months. With one visit, he cured me completely and the pain never returned. From that time onwards I gradually realised I had this power myself whenever I tuned to Spirit. I found I could cure headaches, toothaches, knee and leg problems. Recently, I had an extraordinary experience. I was trying to help my wife Jo's tinnitus, and suddenly we both heard a loud crack simultaneously, whilst I also saw a blue flash like a mini bolt of lightning. Jo's tinnitus disappeared instantly. I'm not making this up!

In the next pavilion dream I met a martial arts master, who simply said, "Don't panic, sport is good". I realised the need to make myself physically strong to accelerate creativity and sharpen focus.

Back home in London I kept up running, swimming and plenty of exercise. My close friends, tremendous character Ralph Bates and his lovely wife Virginia helped me to find my centre by encouraging me to de-stress and have fun. They were both actors. Ralph had starred in many Hammer horror movies amongst other things, and Virginia also ran an extraordinary antique clothes shop in Holland Park. They were incredibly friendly and welcomed me in on their Sunday afternoon gatherings.

When I was alone at home I felt privileged to be invited into their extended family, a cast of colourful characters including Tommy Cooper and also Jimmy Sangster who produced and directed many Hammer horror films which had excited my young mind all those years ago at the old Biograph cinema in Victoria.

Rubbing shoulders with Jon Finch, it was Polanski's

Macbeth meets Hitchcock's *Frenzy*… With a mix of writers, actors and media people, amazing stories were told, red wine flowed freely into and around the glasses, whilst guests sometimes ended up under the table reciting Shakespeare, collapsing into fits of giggles... An all-day affair and a fantastic circus of the absurd. I felt particularly at home here... *Poldark* meets *Dr Jekyll and Sister Hyde* in a theatre of dreams. I was coming back to myself.

By 1982 I'd reached a point where I no longer wanted to capitulate to commercial pressures. I was uncomfortable with the push to turn me into a pop star. I decided to return to my real self, whatever the cost. I was determined the next album must have integrity, my own idiosyncratic stamp, and a harder edge. If Dracula could rise again from the grave, so could I and once more I was out for blood. I couldn't live on red wine alone.

Highly Strung had all the experimental elements that *Cured* lacked. I was still feeling my way in a difficult and mercurial climate, but a track I'm particularly proud of from that time is 'Camino Royale', which I re-recorded recently on *Genesis Revisited II*. It came from a dream where I was with early Genesis and we were playing at our best. I remember the dream well... I was in New Orleans at the time and I'd been walking through the streets of the French Quarter at 3am. I relived the same experience in the dream, shutters rattling in the wind with the sound of distant jazz bands plus a calliope organ from a paddle steamer on the Mississippi. Suddenly I was catapulted forwards as if fired from a gun, shooting out of the street through the swing doors of a wailing fairground ghost train. The ride took me through a neon archway into a theatre where I was rehearsing with Genesis. I was back with them, strangely playing in the audience and on stage at the same time, as I had done for real when I'd wanted to check how the band sounded and looked under the lights. The band was playing that syncopated but anthemic music typical of our style around 1972. I incorporated this into 'Camino Royale'. It intrigued me because it was a combination of so many styles — swinging jazz, with strains of the Old South creeping in. In the song itself I fused these ideas with Nick Magnus' melodic chord driven lines. I felt it was one of the most successful of our co-writes. I enjoyed re-recording it in recent times and would love to do a version with a real orchestra one of these days...

New Orleans has always fascinated me. The French Quarter seems as if it exists outside time. The real and imagined blended together. Its blue notes wailing into the night, its ghostly apparitions, celebrated vampires, cursing voodoo queens concocting spells... An endlessly rich seam to plunder in song, novels, film and theatre...

On my last visit about twenty years back when I was playing at a convention there, I fell victim to its dark side, but yet again ended up with an extraordinary dream. Guitar tech Richard Buckland and I decided to take a ride on the swamps on one of those high-powered hydrofoils. When we set out everything was fine, but a storm quickly brewed up and I ended up swallowing spray whipped up from the slimy depths. Shortly afterwards, I went down with the notorious Swamp Fever. I was massively sick with this for more than a week. Finally, I had a dream where I heard the most sublime music with a woman's soprano voice singing. It was like the parting of clouds. As I heard this, I was even aware in the dream that the pain was subsiding in my stomach. Talk about the magical healing power of music...

8

A galleon on the ever-changing tide...

Sadly, despite 'Cell 151', the hit single from *Highly Strung*, it was my final album on Charisma Records. I had a bad feeling the day I discovered that Malcolm McLaren was acting as a consultant at Charisma. I knew this wasn't good news as they were listening to him and suggesting that this great swindler had good ideas.

The enemy was on the prowl, closing in. It had now infiltrated my closest musical family in the corridors of Charisma itself, which was in some disarray in the face of punk. Plus, not everyone in my team saw eye-to-eye with the record company, which then decided to stop releasing my records. My relationship with them was finally ending.

This saddened me. For all those years I'd had a firm friendship with the top guy at Charisma, Strat, who had been a great support and inspiration. I was very unhappy that long standing association was now coming to an end. Those fun days at the Speakeasy we'd shared were long gone and the camaraderie between us had now been undermined.

He'd known that we would make it before we realised in the early days. The last time I'd had a really great conversation with him was at the Milton Keynes reunion only one year earlier. Just before we were all about to leave, I noticed a figure standing in the shadows. It was Strat. We hugged each other, talked about old times and agreed that the magic of the Milton Keynes concert kicked in precisely as Pete sang the opening lines, "Can you tell me where my country lies…"

Strat was a lovely guy and a visionary who knew how to provide a fertile climate for acts to flower. I'll always remember him with a great deal of love. Later in 1987, when I attended his memorial, so many luminaries from both music and film were there to honour him. Afterwards at the Marquee we all raised our glasses to a remarkable man.

Brian Gibbon from Charisma offered to manage me, which helped me find a way through the blocks and difficulties for my next musical sojourn.

By this time, I'd already recorded several acoustic tracks and Brian found an outlet in the newly formed Lamborghini Records, who liked the idea of a classical guitar album. This was *Bay of Kings*. I'd gradually amassed tracks over several years, and now I finished the album in London's Dickensian Clerkenwell. My love of classical music with the kind of tone Segovia possessed in his guitar playing has always needed an outlet.

Recording went smoothly apart from one unfortunate incident. I was recording the *Bay Of Kings* title track at London's Townhouse Studios. Whilst half-way through, I wanted to check the sound in the control room. In my haste, I crashed headlong into the plate glass door, smashing both my nose and hand, whilst the glass on the door was completely written off, looking as if a bullet had shattered it! I fell backwards and briefly passed out. John Acock rushed in, concerned and told me I needed to go to hospital. But I was determined to finish the recording as I felt the quality of the playing was damn near perfect. So, I carried on. I still feel it's one of the best sounding tracks I've ever done, so it was worth it. A violent moment for such a serene piece of music! When I arrived home, I drowned my pain with a large bottle of Scotch.

I realised I needed to move forward with honesty, energy and inspiration, knowing it was important not to underestimate the powers of the spirit. Having tried several approaches, I'd reached the point where I felt the best thing was to follow my own path, whether that meant commercial success or not. I'd continue to "strive beyond existing stagnant music forms". The tyranny of the ordinary was back with a vengeance, but I was determined to swim against that tide. I'd continue to fight against musical prejudice, to "see no ships" and walk through walls when necessary.

To get to grips with all aspects of music in my aim to break down those boundaries, I decided to immerse myself in completely different styles, from percussion driven rock to classical guitar.

On visits to Brazil I almost felt sympathy with the dreaded punks listening to the Bossa Nova style of music which seemed to have no emotion, no anger... I remember virtually falling asleep to that somnambulant sound in various top restaurants. But through the night air outside you could hear the distant thudding of jungle drums... Sometimes loud and bold and other times cut back to a compellingly quiet insistent tapping like jungle chatter.

I was drawn to the extraordinary rhythms that had grown up in the poverty-ridden favelas. The tribal heart of Africa was still beating there... the same raw spirit behind the essence of rock. I wanted to get that magical sound on an album and started to befriend some of those percussionists, who agreed to record with me. My friend Richard Court who'd become a huge star out there lent me equipment. Nick Magnus flew over and we worked together with the local musos on various rhythms. Often we had to find a common language and make it fast and loose, record it and sort it out later… ethnic meets high tech. Spontaneity ruled the day, or rather the night.

All night sessions were the only thing on offer at Rio's Son Livre studios. I couldn't stay awake at first. I finally succumbed to offers of cocaine helping me to get through those sunless hours. After a while my body stopped telling me I was tired. It was a dangerous combination of cocaine by night and running around the Lagoa lake by day. I wanted to fulfil professional commitments but the price of that was white powder meets green face. It was pure abuse. I didn't normally take cocaine and it didn't exactly agree with me.

The final thing that convinced me cocaine was a really bad idea was one particularly dangerous experience. Again, it was in Brazil, this time at a lavish party where a guy I knew slipped me a bottle of cocaine with a spoon and recommended I take it. Having done this in the spirit of the moment, a few minutes later my heart started to pound so fast I thought I was going to have a heart attack.

God knows what else it was laced with, but I vowed to myself that if I survived that terrifying experience, I would never touch the stuff again. I've always had a fear of acid and heroin and never touched them because I saw what they did to my first girlfriend Barbara, plus at least two heroin addicts I knew who didn't make it out of their teens. There was plenty I wanted to achieve in music, and that's what drove me. Anything that threatened my dream was a potential enemy. I realised too from early on how you get a natural high from many things, including creative drive, a great gig, travelling the world, the meeting of minds, friendship and the feeling of being in love... experiences that can't be replaced by any drug.

Of course, I loved the total immersion in rhythm Brazil provided with amazing local musicians, but the drug-fuelled moonlit trance wore thin and I was relieved to return to England just about in one piece. At least I now had the raw material which Nick and I processed in London with the calming influence of John Acock and where equipment and technology were more readily available. Part two of the project was put together in West London, where we added tracks such as the relentlessly nightmarish 'Duel', based on the idea of the unseen psychotic truck driver in Spielberg's early film.

I named the album *Till We Have Faces*, the title of a favourite CS Lewis book. That title reflected a need to grow, using every style of music across the spectrum.

Ever since reading *The Chronicles Of Narnia*, I'd been drawn to all of Lewis' work. A few years ago, via our video making pal Paul Gosling and his wife Tracey, Jo and I were thrilled to visit his former home on the edge of Oxford, where his spirit still seems to linger. The very walls hint that other worlds are just a whisper away. We've become great pals with warden Debbie, and we've now visited many times. Lewis' home is always bathed in sunlight, and we also love to explore the nearby nature reserve which inspired his idea of the 'wood between the worlds'. Lewis and Tolkien loved to take a rowing boat out on the largest of several ponds in that enchanted spot.

Back in 1984, creative inspiration from CS Lewis through to John Coltrane was burrowing away at my brain cells. Everything I undertook flew in the face of the current musical climate. Singles and synthesisers led the video parade as the eighties got into its stride. The need to follow my heart drove me to choose the road less travelled. Or so I thought...

It's in all those myths and stories. You've found your niche; you think you've got it all figured out. Then there's a knock on the door, an interruption in the street... An old lady with a red and green apple, an odd man with a pair of red shoes, a fox offering an exciting and successful new life in the theatre. As John Lennon once said, "Life is what happens to you when you're making other plans..."

One day, as I was minding my own business dreaming up a new solo project, I was approached by Asia's manager Brian Laine, who felt a collaboration between two guitarists of some standing could be very strong. I was between projects without a new, clearly formed plan, my current label Lamborghini Records was already folding, and I was looking for a new break. A joint guitarist project sounded promising. Newly departed from Asia, Steve Howe liked the idea too... Thus, was born GTR.

While I was working on the GTR album, Tony Banks came to dinner. I told him I was working with Steve Howe and he asked, "Will it come to anything?" That kind of question is a great spur to not only bring something to fruition, but to make it into a real success.

It wasn't easy, as both Steve Howe and I individually had strong ideas which didn't always concur and we ended up over spending on the album... But there was an upside. We were a guitar maker's dream which generated tons of publicity, the tour played to sell-out crowds in the States, 'When The Heart Rules The Mind' became a big hit single and the album went gold. GTR wasn't sustainable, but it was a success!

MTV was playing GTR on the hour, giving us an

enormous level of exposure. Suddenly. Even fourteen-year-old girls were writing fan letters to me. I'd never experienced that before. It shows the power of the media when you get to ride on the crest of that gigantic wave bringing your ship into shore.

To this day I've remained on good terms with the other band members. Talented keyboard player / GTR producer Geoff Downes with his wife Marti often meet Jo and me, and we share jokes about outrageous characters we've known. Steve Howe and I invariably enjoy talking about music when we meet, and I'll forever admire his innovation.

During the GTR period I got to connect with other guitarists as well, including Jeff Beck, David Gilmour, Hank Marvin and Eric Clapton at a get together wishing Hank bon voyage on his forthcoming relocation to Australia.

Hank was a true gentleman and genuinely pleased that so many of us were there to wish him well. For me it felt like things had gone full circle, as The Shadows' 'Man of Mystery' was the first record I ever bought as a kid. On that day it felt great to be in the company of those guys who had so inspired me through my childhood and teens… It felt like we'd all become a band of brothers.

Another muso I met at this time was Bob Geldof who I bumped into at a bash in Bermuda where the island had raised some £40,000 for Live Aid. I complimented Bob on his extraordinary achievement, which the Ethiopians still appreciate to this day. When I visited the country with Jo in early 2019, Bob was still a big hero to them. We saw for ourselves just how bad the poverty is and how much still needs to be done to help them. We bought many basic supplies such as pens for school kids who can't afford either pens or paper and have to spend half the week helping their parents in the fields to survive, but it all felt like a drop in the ocean and we have an ongoing commitment to help them. It certainly does haunt you when you see people struggling against the most overwhelming odds.

So, after GTR, where to go next? There'd been some fantastic exposure with that band, drawing plaudits from Pete Townshend amongst others... It was a springboard to do something special and potentially unique. I knew extraordinary Brian May of Queen, who suggested we work together on a project. This was a very emotionally rewarding marriage of ideas between two guitarists. We liked each other's work, along with Nick Magnus' fab keys. Although Brian had to leave for the States before we'd finished recording, it was still possible to create an album with some extra material. Bonnie Tyler added her magic voice...

Musically it was the best combination yet, and I felt I'd found another holy grail. It was less commercial, and more home grown than GTR, therefore closer to my heart, but it was just as dynamic, and we were poised for success once more... By 1987 it was ready for lift-off. It seemed to have everything going for it. I was confident that with this terrific project my team would find us a great record deal...

But it was not to be. I was told that there weren't any record companies who were offering the right deal. I had to forget it at the time and it eventually came out as *Feedback '86* in 2000.

By mid-1987 I felt there was only one thing I could solidly rely on. My own fingers. For the first time since *Bay of Kings* I turned my attention back to my trusty acoustic guitar. It was an area I could draw strength from when the world seemed to be at odds with me, and a way to keep up my own momentum... Hence the title of my next album, the nylon guitar-based *Momentum*. I came to believe that maybe all I did need, as my Dad once put it, was "A bed, a chair and a guitar". I spent many hours alone in the house and studio developing those classically inspired ideas which I loved. Introspective but lyrical, I was proud of the album... particularly 'The Sleeping Sea'. It came out in 1988, along with an accompanying tour, with brother John once again working his magic flute.

My team had changed by this time. By 1987 Brian Gibbon was no longer managing me as he had started up his own record label. Billy Budis was phased in as my manager. Billy had been sound engineer at several of my shows and he'd become my personal road manager when I toured with GTR in 1986. He had a confident manner, so I guessed he would take to the job. He was to continue as my manager until 2008.

The future was as clear as mud. This was the worst time and I couldn't any longer see a straight path. I spent many hours alone thinking, walking, cycling, running... wondering which way to go. I figured it was time to pay something back. I knew I'd been very lucky in an unequal world.

At that time, I befriended Sean Marriott, a guy with vision who cared greatly about social issues. Together we came up with the idea of a musical charity project. I was concerned when I got to hear about the plight of the Vietnamese boat people who were being turned away from Hong Kong, and Sean offered to help me develop the idea of a musical charity project which became *Rock Against Repatriation*. We devoted the next year to this project, raising money for the boat people cause and involved several well-known musicians and personalities including Justin Hayward, Peter Gabriel and Tom Conti. It was even on the UK news on Christmas Day.

The time was right to do something to help, and Sean worked all hours around the clock to help on this project. But unfortunately, according to Billy it wasn't possible to find a record deal for an album from this project apart from one company that had bounced cheques, so at this point the project ended.

As the 1980s came to a close, the future was unclear. Record deals now felt like a distant dream. I spent loads of time alone at home wondering what to do and which way to turn. This was a challenging time. By early 1990 the old internal invalidator was knocking on the door. There'd been no record deal or tour since 1988. I was once again suffering from the paralysis of fear where you're held down by invisible chains.

I developed stage fright. It gained such a firm grip that I had to see a doctor for hypnotism to be able to do a one-off show for Central TV. The last straw was when I played with the London Chamber Orchestra. I'd just done a decent rendition of a Vivaldi piece when surprising me out of the blue, orchestra leader Christopher Warren-Green turned to the audience and said, "Would you like to hear some of Steve's music now?" Because it took everything out of me to overcome my nerves playing Vivaldi, I started to struggle as I played my own nylon guitar stuff. My nerves continued to rage away like an internal earthquake as I came off stage and I realised I'd developed a severe case of stage fright, not experienced since my earliest shows with Genesis. My confidence was rocked and I continued to feel the tremors for many weeks. I finally saw a sympathetic hypnotherapist who asked me to discuss my problem at length. He then said, "We only concentrate on positives". I didn't realise when he hypnotised me that I was under the spell of this practitioner, who reminded me how good I was at my work. I burst into tears and apologised to him afterwards, saying, "I'm sorry, it must be unusual for someone to react like this." He surprised me by replying, "It's actually very common indeed when you are successfully hypnotised because you're very relaxed and you no longer have the usual emotional blocks." He showed me how to self-hypnotise and suggested I use the knowledge before future shows, which I did. Needless to say, these days I don't need to do that anymore. My confidence is restored.

Early in the New Year of 1990 via Zomba Music I received a film script to read with a view to compose music for it. I loved the script, which was written by Joanna Lehmann, who was to become my wife just over twenty years later. Jo and her team met me to discuss it. She and I worked on the idea of a fantasy film called *Soulscapes*, a fascinating project driven by music and visuals.

Jo gave me a lot of encouragement and helped me regain confidence. I directed a pilot for it and created the music. Composing music for a film project widened my horizons as it gave me the opportunity to explore sonic areas I hadn't touched before. The music touched many zones, highlighting drama, atmosphere, suspense, joy, fear, threat and ran the gamut of emotions. Directing the pilot was also an extraordinary experience, working with actors and a whole team of film makers. It felt refreshing and liberating to do something totally different. Exploring emotional, atmospheric and visual elements together linked with my approach to music and helped broaden my musical horizons further... During that pilot, I directed Dexter Fletcher, who recently did a great job himself directing the film *Rocket Man* about the life of Elton John.

At this point I realised how important it was to keep moving. I decided to put a band together and hit the road... Julian Colbeck, who I was soon to work with as well on recordings, joined on keyboards. He'd worked extensively with the Yes guys. He was a great character who was able to improvise brilliantly. We've remained pals to this day. Dave Ball on bass had a furiously fast bass slapping technique which brought the house down every night. Hugo Degenhardt was a fantastic fiery young drummer, who has since played Ringo in the Bootleg Beatles... This was a rootsy tour of North America, back to the clubs.

A short while later, we also played South America. The tour went smoothly until Hugo went swimming in the sea off Copacabana Beach, Rio. He was hit by an unexpectedly powerful wave which hurled him down to the seabed, dislocating his shoulder. At a moment's notice, local drummer Sergio bravely agreed to learn the whole set overnight. At the gig the following night, Sergio played drums alongside Hugo, still impressive drumming up a storm with just one arm!

I was determined to release another album, whether there was full support from a record company or not. I'd amassed material and it was nearly five years since the release of *Momentum*. *Guitar Noir* came out in 1993. Much of the album was introspective, but that was how I'd often felt for a while by that time. That approach worked for me particularly well with the track 'Dark as the Grave', with its mysterious atmosphere. It was a personal song too because I was mourning the death of my dear friend Ralph Bates, who'd recently died far too young.

Another poignant piece was 'There are Many Sides to the Night', inspired by an observation of women whose lives are compromised by circumstance and in particular that lady of the night I had once spoken to over breakfast. But despite the generally dark tone, you could never totally keep a Hackett in that place of shadows... The sun sometimes burst through in a big way, as with 'Sierra Quemada' with its sweeping guitar, that moment of rising above everything and flying into the sky. I toured this album with almost the same team, but now with Doug Sinclair on bass. He and Hugo were a hugely dynamic rhythm section. Doug was able to tap on bass whilst playing Taurus pedals with his feet.

The urge gripped me to do something fun to help counteract that inward state of mind. I'd long since stopped battling to maintain a profile. By now I was just trying to keep my sanity and stay afloat. A new idea came to me. I allowed both guitar and harmonica to let rip for my album *Blues with a Feeling*, reigniting the blues passion of my teens and tearing away some of those cobwebs that had wound their way around my brain.

It reconnected me to that time when life was a relatively simple open book with all those pages yet to be filled... a time when my personal world was young and so much felt new and fresh. Off with the shackles! It reawakened memories of the Stones, Paul Butterfield and Cream as godlike bands and Eel Pie Island as Mecca.

It was great to reacquaint with the harmonica. I'd always admired Larry Adler, possibly the most famous harmonica player in the world. I'd been a fan ever since I was a kid learning harmonica and was glad to get to meet him. Larry played a mean version of 'Rhapsody in Blue' with left hand on the piano and right hand on the harmonica. He recalled how his pal George Gershwin had preferred the harmonica version to the more famous orchestral version. In the right hands, that little expressive instrument can be a whole orchestra in itself!

Some people are adept at blowing their own trumpet in a different way... On the same evening after meeting

Larry I bumped into Ivana Trump. She introduced me to sixteen-year-old Ivanka, who was quietly observing whilst her mother was busily working the room, sizing up everyone and their status in film, music and society. Later I was sucked into an Ivana birthday celebration, where a ballroom had been hired for the occasion. When Ivana heard her 'introduction' music being played by the function band in the inner sanctum, she shouted, "Oh, I'm supposed to be on stage for that!" She rapidly pushed me and about ten others out of the way to make it through the doors for her big moment. Drinks were spilled, waiters dropped trays, but hors d'ouvres had to be obeyed while we desperately tried to make way for that hairdo, redolent of Patsy in *Absolutely Fabulous*.

Next stop after the Blues Train… On the occasions I toured during the early to mid-nineties I felt more open to possibilities. Just after one show in Sicily a fan nervously asked me if I would mind signing his Genesis albums. I was surprised he thought that would bother me. As I thought further about it on the plane back to London, it dawned on me that not only did I still love the music I played with Genesis, but I would love to re-record some of those wonderful songs. So the idea of *Genesis Revisited* was born.

With that first *Genesis Revisited* album, although I wanted to remain true to the original spirit, I felt the need to make several changes. I wanted to feel free to reinterpret the past. I had radical sounds I wanted to employ, and I felt a need to put my own stamp on it. It was a chance to express my own take on music that had been a group effort.

These changes are obvious on both 'Firth of Fifth' and 'Your Own Special Way'. This was a different time to the recent *Genesis Revisited II* album where my interpretations were closer to the original songs. I think in recent times

I've explored and developed my own music so much that I felt less of a need to make big changes. With the more recent album, I just wanted to build on the original spirit of each track with the knowledge and experience I now have, plus the technical capabilities of today, along with extra orchestral textures.

The original *Genesis Revisited* album came out in 1996. I then put together a band comprising John Wetton, Ian McDonald, Chester Thompson, Julian Colbeck and myself to perform in Japan playing numbers from Genesis, Asia and King Crimson. It came out as the live album *The Tokyo Tapes*.

To be in the Land of the Rising Sun for the first time was like landing on a whole other planet. I loved Kyoto, with its golden temples, water gardens and stunning shrines. On a recent visit, Jo and I felt particularly uplifted by the Inari Mountain Shinto shrine leading you on a spiritual journey up through a thousand deep red gateways...

All of us in the band were intrigued by the huge contrasts of old world and ultra-modern Tokyo. We were in a large new hotel where Michael Jackson was also staying. Every time he descended into the lobby, he was instantly surrounded by a hundred people and a film camera followed his every move. He only ever made it half-way across the lobby, then gave up and returned to his room. I wouldn't want to have that level of fame. A prisoner of his own popularity... a life in the gilded goldfish bowl.

It was knockout to work with such an extraordinary team of high achievers on *Genesis Revisited* and *The Tokyo Tapes*.

Whenever I get really involved with rock, my acoustic side always hops up and screams out to be heard! My next project was *A Midsummer Night's Dream*. In the early stages whilst I was playing an acoustic guitar track I had recorded to Jo, she commented that it brought to mind the Shakespeare play *A Midsummer Night's Dream*. I decided to develop several tracks for that theme, culminating with 'Celebration'. Many people have since used that track for their weddings, including Jo and me for ours!

EMI took on *A Midsummer Night's Dream*, released in 1997, the Royal Philharmonic Orchestra played wonderfully on it, arranged and conducted by my cousin Matt Dunkley.

People often twin *A Midsummer Night's Dream* with *Metamorpheus*, which came out a few years later in 2005. Both albums used a twin combo of acoustic guitar with orchestra. I loved doing this as I've always been fascinated by that instrumental combination. Both albums also followed the theme of a known mythological tale.

Metamorpheus is a more universal story and was a challenge to orchestrate. This was the first time I had to recreate a chase, a death, an underworld journey, the pain of loss and a violent murder through my version of classical music and playing, which had until this time been almost solely a peaceful alternative to rock. It was also a fascinating challenge to imitate Orpheus' harp with guitar.

I developed several compositions for *Metamorpheus* at Jo's home. Her guidance was invaluable. Jo's love and knowledge of Greek mythology enabled me to bring *Metamorpheus* to life and tackle some of the more thematic aspects. We went into all those huge questions of life and death, death and rebirth in spirit, and how light and darkness are intertwined. We explored Orpheus' link to both Apollo god of light and the dark irrational god Dionysos, plus how the Maenads who destroyed Orpheus, transformed into the Muses who mourned him, honouring his spirit. Years later in 2014 Jo and I found the magical centre of the Apollo and Dionysos cult where the Delphic oracle began.

The remote Corycian Cave is reached by a perilous rocky dirt track on the side of Mount Parnassos near Delphi in Greece. The cave's mythology and powerful primitive atmosphere inspired the track 'Corycian Fire' on my relatively recent album *Wolflight*. It felt like finally following Orpheus into the Underworld and bringing his journey back out to the light.

With 'Corycian Fire', I explored the overlap of rock and classical styles, orchestral and choral sounds enhancing and firing off electric guitar salvos. If violin strings are pure spirit, rock guitar has an earthy, brassy quality. Together they can both sound like the human cry. It's an endless quest to emulate the power of emotion, with an unearthly supernatural edge.

Back in the mid-1990s, I was sad to lose Julian Colbeck, who moved to the States after the gigs in Japan. We'd done some great stuff together by that point. But then two invaluable and extraordinary guys came into my working life...

Ben Fenner became involved as recording engineer. He had strong input on *Genesis Revisited*. Multi-talented Ben had worked extensively with Brian Eno and The Cranberries amongst many others. His sonic sculptures are extraordinary on both his sound engineering and recording work with me. He's a fine musician too and a mean guitar player. In more recent times, he's also created beautiful music with his talented composer / musician fiancé, Leslie Bennett.

Roger King joined my team just before the *Genesis Revisited* recordings which he worked on as well as Ben... Roger started out as very quiet and polite, but familiarity soon brought out the horns of his spikey sense of humour, as dry as the Sahara Desert. You know that you've gained his full respect and friendship once you've become a victim of his sharp observations… I always get the unvarnished truth from him, which I value. Whatever he turns his hand to is brilliant. His ear for detail is exceptional and he turns musical doodles into masterful portraits. He's also an amazing keyboard player. I'm hugely honoured to have him on board with the band on keys and as musical director, as well as his engineering and co-writing.

I no longer think reincarnation is likely, but I often muse on the fact that Roger reminds me of Bach. Likewise, Nick Magnus brings Tchaikovsky to mind, whilst Tony Banks has something of Beethoven about him. All three keyboard players seem to share temperament, physical characteristics and talents respectively with those three extraordinary musical luminaries.

Having done a fantastic job engineering *A Midsummer Night's Dream,* in early 2000 Roger worked tirelessly with me on the *Sketches of Satie* album alongside John on flute. Both John and I had always been entranced by the haunting strains of Erik Satie's music. It was a labour of love for us all.

In the summer of 2000, Roger joined me on tour playing keys for the first time. Roy Castle's son Ben took on woodwind and brass. He was a great multi-instrumentalist and hilariously funny, just like his exceptionally talented pal Rob Townsend, who was shortly to take over on all things blown. Gary O'Toole also became a part of the band at that time. Like Phil, as well as being a great drummer, he also had a super singing voice, used beautifully on his rendition of 'Blood on the Rooftops'. We were joined by fab bass player Phil Mulford as well, who on the next tour was followed by the equally gifted Terry Gregory.

At the time Rob joined us in 2000, we headed off to South America. This tour wasn't without incident. The promoter hadn't organised Brazilian visas, so we missed some shows before finally getting in there. The band went to the consulate and I became so agitated that I lost my temper and was escorted off the premises at gunpoint! Sometimes, the pressure had been so much that we'd let our hair down on a day off.

In Mexico, having drunk far too much at a tasting session, I climbed up the Pyramid of the Moon at Teotihuacan... I wobbled about precariously at the top in a tequila infused stupor. Terrified I'd fall, I descended the whole thing on all fours. All I lost was injured pride and a fingernail. Luckily, it was the end of the tour.

From 2000, most of my albums were issued via InsideOut, which continues to release them today. I have a terrific working relationship with them. Over the last ten years, sales of my albums have shot up along with the invaluable support and guidance of Thomas Waber, David Gulvin, Freddy Palmer, Stefan Franke and others in the company, alongside Jo, myself, Roger and terrific, unstoppable whirlwind Sharon Chevin, who has been my publicist since around 2000.

Returning back to 1999, my first original rock album since 1993, *Darktown* was released. Like *Guitar Noir* it had an introspective element, but it took many unexpected turns. By this time, I wanted to go out on a limb more with a variety of moods and influences and to get into some of those dark areas which are often avoided. It contained more anger than the previous album and it was more intimate.

Darktown included personal memories, as with 'Jane Austen's Door', which was a gentler view of my first girlfriend than 'Every Day'. I had recently met Barbara again after many years and I realised how she'd become severely diminished through the choices she had made which had compromised her life. She'd had so much potential as a young girl. My anger at the way she had treated me had by now turned to sadness on her behalf.

Other tracks like 'Dreaming with Open Eyes' were more experimental. Both this one and 'Golden Age of Steam' were inspired by dreams. Ben Fenner created an amazing driving orchestral sound on 'Golden Age of Steam', using his strong sense of drama and pace.

'Rise Again' was partly inspired by a piece of Native American poetry, but also linked to personal feelings, most strongly expressed in metaphor. Sometimes life makes you feel like the bad guy outcast, but you know you're following your heart and your feelings are valid. You turn defiant and hoist that pirate sail again. *Darktown* was largely based on my unhappy school experiences. It was cathartic to give expression to the trauma. Jo, who'd also suffered at school wrote a poem which formed the basis for the first part of the song.

By contrast, *To Watch the Storms* (2003) had a lighter feel (except for the sudden burst of anger in 'Mechanical Bride'!) I wasn't exploring my feelings and inner universe so much at that time. I was coasting, gaining inspiration from books, places I had visited over the years, along with my interest in the outer reaches of both the world and the mind, shown in 'Silk Road' and 'Frozen Statues'.

The final rock album from this period was *Wild Orchids* (released in 2006). By now personal anxieties were bubbling under the surface. The album had a Gothic atmosphere. I felt particularly proud of 'Downstreet' and 'Wolfwork', both of which had quirky originality alongside underlying savagery. When fears are kept under wraps, they often find expression through dark comedy and metaphor. Life was about to take a different turn…

9

A new sun rises on the road ahead...

Increasingly, Kim and I both needed to lead separate personal lives. By 2007 Jo and I had become very close. We were writing more lyrics and musical ideas together. Our love had become so strong and I realised we had found a soul mate in each other. However, I was very nervous of the potential upheaval of divorce.

Initially, when I moved out of the house in early 2007 Jo and I stayed in a log cabin in Tilford Woods. Roger joined us there to record 'Fantasy', which finally came out on *Beyond the Shrouded Horizon*. I think Jo's and my temporary time there was subliminally reflected in that song, which we wrote together. Two other songs we wrote that were influenced by that situation were 'Nomads' on *Out of the Tunnel's Mouth* and 'Between the Sunset and the Coconut Palms' on *Shrouded*. We felt like gypsies or refugees, without a solid base. It was a strange atmosphere, surrounded by woods in the winter snow.

But the real world still had to be faced... Hansel and Gretel had to grow up for survival and return home to face a lot more than just the music. The final stages of the divorce were put into motion in April 2007. Anxious to find a peaceful way through, I moved into a flat on my own. I went through a lot of emotional trauma, which comes out in the lyrics of 'Fire on the Moon' on *Out of the Tunnel's Mouth*. I was in a state of turmoil and confusion.

Once again, I'd reached that point where the door of change needed to be gone through and I realised that there was something positive beckoning beyond those terrors of the dark unknown. The time had come to stop being controlled by conflicting emotions, to move forward and take the reins of my life. It was very distressing for Jo to be living alone again. Kim's and my divorce came through in May 2007. Around that time, I asked Jo to join me in the apartment.

In 2008 I forged ahead with a new business situation, taking on self-management with the invaluable and unwavering support of my new team involving Jo, Brian Coles, Roger King and Amanda Lehmann.

For legal reasons, I wasn't sure if circumstances would enable me to tour at that time. But then, a terrific thing happened. Whilst attending a convention in the atmospheric Italian hilltop town of Orvieto in the autumn of 2008, across a crowded corridor Jo and I recognised Vania Santi of Blue Sky Agency. She had taken care of my touring team for some years in Italy. She had wondered what was happening and drove several hours across the country to find out. On hearing about my situation, she was concerned and spoke to Sergio Fornasari who ran Blue Sky. The next thing we knew was an offer of an Italian tour.

In early 2009 I went back on the road. This was the first time I'd been out with a full rock show in about five years. Vania, Sergio and his wife Patty have become close friends of ours and we love to visit them all in Cesena and we hook up with Vania whenever we can. Vania has introduced us to some of the most unusual and special places in Italy.

Jo and I had a wonderful holiday with her a short while back in Southern Italy, visiting both a ghost town and the extraordinary Matera, a town of cave houses cut into the rock.

Following that Italian tour, agents and promotors in other countries came up with offers, and with Brian Coles' help, my touring career was once again up and running. It was a great band line up, including Roger King, Rob Townsend, Gary O'Toole and newcomer to the team, Nick Beggs.

On the road, Rob and Roger have always had us all in stitches of laughter with their double act of horrendous mutual insults. Rob has a huge array of alter-egos, from Alabama road rat Diesel Dawg when he gets behind the band van wheel in the USA, to the oily vicar in the UK replete with false teeth, to the fanged velvet vampire of Prague... Multi-skilled Rob can turn his hand to any wind instrument and takes on every challenge with extraordinary dexterity.

Equally talented bass, twelve string and stick player Nick Beggs always held everyone's attention with his powerful musicianship, as well as his spontaneous desire to remove his clothes. The first time was on a snowy Yorkshire moorland when we all commented on the cold except Nick, who stripped himself naked, shouting out, "No it's not... I'm free, I'm free!" as he trotted off into the wilds... After the fun and games, they'd all play an absolute blinder of a gig, which helped to lift my spirits in what was otherwise a personally traumatic time.

To avoid potential legal challenges, I recorded at home instead of in the studio. Most of what was to become *Squackett* and *Out of the Tunnel's Mouth* was recorded in the living room of my apartment. I was incredibly relieved to discover that it was possible to do this! We were still able to create fully-fledged, uncompromised albums even if it was best to wait for a while to release them. The support I received from Jo in particular, also family, friends and fans meant an enormous amount to me and kept me from falling over the mental and emotional precipice that often threatened to swallow me up.

The legal situation linked to the divorce was finally settled in court, November 2010.

I believe that often when you experience psychological trauma, if you get through it you grow as a person. I came out of it knowing I'd gained a whole new level of strength. I no longer listen to that inner voice of doom. It was like finally growing up and getting a second chance. And what an amazing feeling it was to be back in the studio and free to forge full steam ahead!

Now everything feels possible. I can take on anything with a sense of empowerment... I appreciate the autonomy and freedom I have. Jo is a huge support and it's great to have mutual respect and a fab working relationship with the team. We're like a big family.

Brian Coles organises touring, Amanda Lehmann the website, Adrian Holmes the webstore, merch and tour management.

Ben Fenner has been amazing right the way through as both sound mixer at live gigs and as engineer for several of my recordings, as well as the many hours of work he has put into most of the live DVDs.

Multi-talented Roger King is musical director as well as co-writer, keyboard player, programmer and engineer on my studio albums. Andrea Holmes produces those beautiful tour programmes and Angéla and Maurizio Vicedomini have created those amazing art photos for several of the albums. Michael Diner is our much-needed accountant!

Jo and I are at the hub of the team. We discuss all ideas together, and Jo runs the business as a central coordinator / co-manager. Jo works for long hours every day and it's terrific to see her dedication. Jo and I also write tons of the music together along with Roger King. With her musical family background, Jo comes up with lyrics and melody lines, many of which I employ. I'll discuss all aspects of the songs as they progress with both Jo and Roger.

Over the years we have also had firm support of close friends, such as Harry Pearce, who has designed several of my album covers and booklets, and also works with Pete Gabriel on his Witness projects. Nick Clabburn, who was originally at school with my brother was always there for Jo and me. A great friend to this day, Nick sometimes joins us on the road or on holiday. He's also an excellent lyricist in his own right, having written all the lyrics for two of John's albums, and with us on the songs 'Divided Self' and 'Sleepers'. He and Ant Phillips are pals too, and the wit they both share can often have Jo and me in stitches when we all get together.

Jo is a consistently loving wife, there for me in every way. It's terrific to have a creative partner who shares my life and interests. She's stood by me through thick and thin, helping me to see what's achievable with scant regard for her own needs. With Jo by my side, I believe all things are possible, and I feel like the luckiest guy in the world! We find something incredible to experience in every place we visit around the globe on tour and we've made pals everywhere. It's a big circle of friendship and inspiration. I find my music has more ethnic influence through our travels, both on tour and holidays. Exploring many parts of Africa, North and South America, India, the Far East, Australasia, Europe, Scandinavia and Russia together is a fantastic journey of discovery, heightened by the great love we share.

Jo and I married on 4th June 2011. It was a magical day surrounded by close friends and family. Our team and band were there as well, all celebrating together. We felt our dreams had finally come true. In the years that have passed since then, our joy has continued to deepen, and our love is stronger than ever.

The only sadness has been the subsequent tragic loss of several close family members who were all at the wedding such as my dear Dad who had bravely struggled for years with Parkinson's Disease, my wonderful warm Aunt Margaret, Jo's incredibly special, loving mum and Jo's cousin Jeanne who had introduced Jo to the music of Genesis when they were both just fifteen and was Maid of Honour at our wedding. We've also lost several wonderful pals including Chris Squire and John Wetton. I'll always miss them both. I still talk to them in my dreams and we continue to discuss musical ideas together.

John had worked with me in Japan on the tour filmed as *The Tokyo Tapes*, and then in recent years he often joined me as guest on stage as well as featuring on my *Genesis Revisited* albums. We originally met over forty years ago. He was a lovely guy with an incredibly warm heart and a fantastic sense of humour as well as being a great musician and wonderful singer. It had been special to work together with Chris on the Squackett album, *A Life Within a Day*, which involved the ever-talented Roger King along with Chris' songs and mine which we all developed together, as well as numbers we worked on from scratch including the title track 'A Life Within a Day'.

I was always impressed by the power of Chris' bass playing and the way he became one with the instrument, moving with every note. He was a night bird. He'd often show up around 5pm, work into the evening and then we'd go somewhere to eat with Jo and his wife Scotty. They were a tremendously fun couple. The wine would flow and every get together was a celebration. He wasn't very popular with my band one night when he went backstage before the end of a show and drank all the alcohol on their rider! But he was forgiven, as he really was an extraordinary character and one of the world's best bass players. For Squackett, we had a front cover feature on *Prog* magazine. Over the years, Jerry Ewing and the team behind *Prog* Mag have been a great support.

Following *Out of the Tunnel's Mouth*, I decided not to release another album until after the court case had been settled. I accumulated a lot of material, which finally came out as both *A Life Within a Day* and my solo album *Beyond the Shrouded Horizon,* which was less dark than *Tunnel*, but still a strong expression of personal feelings.

It felt great to take songs from the new albums alongside the old with such a talented and charismatic band. Since that time there have been some band changes. It was wonderful to have talented Amanda Lehmann with us around the time of *Tunnel* and *Shrouded*. She added a splendid female element with her beautiful voice and red guitar. I'm always thrilled when she still guests with us on tour.

Extraordinary bass player currently with ELO Lee Pomeroy took over for a while, followed by excellent guitarist / bass player Roine Stolt of the Flower Kings. Now I'm thrilled to have Jonas Reingold on bass with Craig Blundell on drums. What an incredible rhythm section! They both possess extraordinary power and precision. I feel a quickening of the spirit whenever the band takes off and the music flies on stage. All those musicians I've worked with over the years have been brilliant.

As I was finishing this book, I'd just returned from the USA. The band was on fire and even more extraordinary than ever. With the sudden fast spread of Coronavirus, our tour was halted by official directives. It felt incredibly weird. I've never had to stop a tour halfway through before. I was concerned for everyone who couldn't see the show, whilst realising the danger of large gatherings. At least the gigs are postponed, so we will return!

Being on the last flight from Philly to London brought to mind my song, 'Last train to Istanbul'. We were lucky to get back home. Our equipment had to be returned by ship, so that was a slow boat to Liverpool! On return I put out some YouTube music from home to help keep up morale of friends and fans. Important to all stay connected in tough, worrying weeks and to wish everyone well.

With our *Seconds Out* tour plans, we still all had something to look forward to beyond the dark time. Aware of the three-man Genesis reunion plans, I commented that it's great for everyone, for whilst they tend to prioritise the 80s version, I celebrate the 70s Genesis classics.

The special thing about Genesis was the extraordinary music we wrote together and the respect and enthusiasm we received from fans, who have often asked for a reformation. In 2005 all five of us had met in Glasgow to discuss a possible reformation to play some *Lamb* shows. Peter was interested, but there were some differences of approach which led to a decision not to go ahead. Tony, Mike and Phil decided to do a few shows in 2007. I was open to joining, but they wanted those shows to be just the three of them. So, for all those who ask me why we can't all just reform, it's not that simple. It takes five to Tango to do the classic material and the four-man version is not on offer, so I choose to celebrate much of that gorgeous early material, free of politics but with a totally restored spirit.

I felt extraordinarily honoured to be inducted into the hugely important Rock 'n' Roll Hall of Fame in 2010. It was a magic moment at the Waldorf Hotel in New York, where it was terrific to see all our work being celebrated. The band Phish kicked off the evening with a rousing rendition of 'Watcher of the Skies'.

Other acts being inducted included Abba. Benny gave an eloquent speech, with Meryl Streep and Michael Douglas looking on. We had our chance to speak too. At first the evening seemed stiff and formal, but as everyone started to relax, the music flowed with the wine. At one point, Phil went into a Fred Astaire impression, bravely attempting to get Tony to loosen up and dance with him beside the table... Angie Rutherford kindly organised a meal just before the event, where I was able to introduce Jo to all the guys and their wives. At the gathering, Phil was particularly warm and welcoming, which we both really appreciated. It felt as if time had stood still.

Pete couldn't join the R&RHOF induction because of commitments, but Jo and I have met him on several occasions in recent times, particularly in connection with his Witness projects. His social conscience has always been unwavering. It's a joy to see him and have the chance to catch up. The last time we all met together was for the premier of the Genesis Documentary, *Together and Apart*. The documentary celebrated Phil's, Pete's, Mike's and Tony's solo careers whilst ignoring mine, even though the director had interviewed me about it. Later, the director tweeted that Mike had asked for more of his career and less of mine. It was awkward for me, but I was glad to see everyone.

Several of us also joined for the launch of both Mike's

autobiography and that of Richard MacPhail, who has remained a firm pal to this day. Jo and I often meet up with Richard and his incredibly nice professional harpsichord player wife, Maggie Cole. Like Pete and ourselves, they care about everything, from close friends to the state of the wider fragile world today. These days I also enjoy spending time with Ant Phillips, both an incredibly talented musician and a hilarious raconteur. He would have fitted right in there with stable mates at Charisma, the witty Monty Python team.

Even though a reformation still seems unlikely, we all maintain a connection. Over time, we have appreciated each other's work. I remember phoning Mike Rutherford after hearing his first solo album to congratulate him on it, way before Mike and the Mechanics. On another occasion, Tony Banks said he thought 'Shadow of the Hierophant' could have been used by Genesis, and I praised his *A Curious Feeling* album. I let Phil know I enjoyed his *Face Value*, whilst he showed his appreciation of *Please Don't Touch*. Peter liked *Voyage of the Acolyte* and he told me he thought 'Hoping Love Will Last' was outstanding. I was bowled over by his third album (*Peter Gabriel III*). Mike said he wished he'd played on 'Solsbury Hill'. The three of us got to play that song together with my band at a benefit gig for Tadworth Court and the Great Ormond Street Hospital for children.

At gigs I realised just how much fans enjoyed the Genesis music. There were still many Genesis numbers I loved too and longed to cover myself with the addition of orchestra and the advantage of today's technology. I've often marvelled at what was so special about Genesis in the seventies.

Music doesn't exist in splendid isolation. Genesis mixed Shostakovich with Buddy Rich. Had church music previously been allowed to syncopate with the 'Devil's interval'? The notorious flattened fifth was a one-time hanging offence... Suddenly it transforms into a romantic Russian countess found in bed with a vicar (minus dog collar) at the end of the pier!

Music always nails its colours to the mast. In classical circles harmony rules. In rock, drums lead the tribal charge. Luckily with Genesis there were no rules. You could be brutal or sensitive, sometimes in the same song. Genesis had delicacy and power, which was a heady combination. Sharp contrasts ruled the day.

The Mellotron harboured a convincing alien invasion and also became the backdrop to a Greek myth in full flood. Two Mellotron biggies were 'Watcher of the Skies' and 'The Fountain of Salmacis'. The band had a wide frame of references. One day we'd be talking about Judy Collins' 'Wild Flowers' and the next, Miklas Rosza's ramming speed music from *Ben Hur* with the fallen heroes of Respighi's 'Pines Of Rome' in a reanimated procession from the grave, the legions pouring out into the light once more, influencing 'Fly on a Windshield' — a wall of keyboards permeated by guitar screams.

How much improv? How much form versus spirit? Sometimes all of us in Genesis pulled in so many directions at once, it's amazing how we finished those songs that turned battlegrounds of one idealist versus another into fully formed phoenixes, rising from the ashes of conflict.

Then there was the problem of how to put this across live. On 'Supper's Ready' for instance, I felt strongly that the song wouldn't work unless it had everything going for it. "All change!" had to be on tape with the sound of train doors slamming. Pete and I stood shoulder to shoulder on this one as well as all the other sound effects to give the journeying

179

song its best chance.

Why *Genesis Revisited*? I always felt that Genesis was unfinished business. Being a detail freak for me means getting things totally right. 'The Chamber of 32 Doors' for instance would have been great if the original had that extra level of controlled playing and sustain. The guitar needs to be accurate to create anything like the impression of a voice. But I know I got there on the re-recording of that song.

I embarked on the ambitious double album *Genesis Revisited II*, which also involved many wonderful guests, including Chris Squire, Steven Wilson, Nik Kershaw, John Wetton, Steve Rothery and Jakko Jakszyk. Both album and gigs were a great success.

We now had a new addition to the band, fabulous and flamboyant singer Nad Sylvan. He has remained with us ever since as a unique band member with great vocal skills and charismatic presence. With the support of some fantastic agents, including Solo and Kilimanjaro in the UK, plus Entourage Talent in America, along with other agencies and promotors, we globe trot the world with *Genesis Revisited*. A high point for those shows was a packed house at the Royal Albert Hall in London. Shows are once again selling out in terrific venues and albums are charting as they did decades ago.

For some years now I've enjoyed combining Genesis and solo music at shows. It's a combination which we enjoy as much as the fans. It's great to perform songs from both new and old albums as well as the iconic Genesis material from the seventies, loved by so many people.

I'm always up for additional projects. I've guested on a ton of things. Collaborations still fire me up. I've worked with orchestras in UK, Germany, Iceland and the States. It's an amazingly enriching experience with the combination of band and orchestra. Classical music will always be a part of my soul. I enjoy acoustic shows as well as rock gigs and although the solo albums are mainly rock, I continue to write music for acoustic guitar. I also like to wander off the beaten track.

Once a year I join Attila Égerházi's Hungarian band Djabe for mainly Eastern European gigs, although once we all hit Malaysia! It's always a wild adventure touring with Djabe. Once, we played at a strange festival where cows mingled with the crowds in a place called Wolf Village on a Carpathian Mountainside. Midnight arrived and we piled into a vehicle which sped up the mountain to an old crumbling dwelling which looked like the last retreat before Dracula's castle, replete with animal skulls around the walls. There we were given a strange tasting brew around a cracked old wooden table. Unbelievable dreams followed…

The video I did with them for the 'Tears for Peace' song required me to ride through the streets of Budapest in an old army tank shouting through a megaphone in Hungarian… When we meet, the music is equally unpredictable and it's thrilling to explore a combination of rock, jazz, fusion, Eastern European folk, and exotic sounds like the Middle Eastern tar, Moroccan bass and Russian cymbalom. They're all extraordinary musicians and I feel compelled to keep returning to explore their musical world.

I employ influences from my 'safaris' with Djabe on album tracks. I'm now working with other artists who play instruments from far and wide, including the Indian sitar, Arabian oud, Peruvian charango and Australian didgeridoo. I've particularly enjoyed involving musical inspiration, players, singers and instruments from around the world on my most recent three albums, *Wolflight, The Night Siren* and *At The Edge Of Light*.

Travels with Jo to places such as Peru, North Africa, Iceland, USA, India, Australia and the Far East inspired music and lyrics on recent albums. The magic of our visit to Machu Pichu, Peru quickened the spirit, with ideas for the song 'Inca Terra'.

Some places took us to extremes… Iceland in January was exceptionally cold, yet it beckoned you in to its wild and mystical volcanic landscape, giving rise to '50 Miles from the North Pole'… In Jordan, Morocco and Egypt, we felt linked to the ancient world, from the pyramids to Petra, alongside the allure of the golden wilderness, particularly whilst staying in the Arabian desert with Bedouins. All this influenced several tracks, such as 'The Two Faces of Cairo', 'Dust and Dreams' and 'Behind the Smoke'. Vibrant exotica entwined with lurking danger in India with its rivers of life and death inspired 'Shadow and Flame'… And more is to come…

Our recent visit to Ethiopia has given us new ideas for the next project. It felt incredible to sit amongst fifty baboons, to float on a small boat between swimming hippos and basking crocodiles, and to visit some of the world's most ancient underground churches. But most extraordinary of all was our chance to meet remote tribal people of the Rift Valley. They still wear lip plates, horns, tattoos and face paints, they live in tiny straw huts and have spiritual traditions going far back into the mists of time…

Experiences with pals have been invaluable too. 'Under the Eye of the Sun' sprang from the Navaho and Hopi spirit inhabiting Monument Valley and the Painted Desert which we explored with our filming friends Leigh Harris and Franck Avril.

It's an extraordinary life. I've learned you can befriend any creature from practically any species once fear is taken out of the equation. I gave a tiny four inch gecko a grape which it made off with, I've played with a male lion and with wolves too.

For the album cover of *Wolflight*, thanks to a contact via our art photography pals Angéla and Maurizio Vicedomini in Italy, we spent a whole day with real wolves, holding their cubs and communicating in a way I never thought possible. They're incredibly intelligent creatures, and I can see how they would have been powerful totems for tribes of the distant past.

For both *The Night Siren* and *At The Edge of Light*, I worked with people from all over the world. I was thrilled to involve a Palestinian with an Israeli on *The Night Siren*. Serbian director Ivan Colic directed an amazing video for my song 'Behind the Smoke' about the plight of refugees. I feel strongly that rather than hiding behind our borders, we should build bridges between nations and embrace all our differences. Music crosses borders. Diversity is the life-force...

Musically, I'm particularly proud of the most recent album, *At The Edge Of Light*, with creative involvement from Roger and Jo, plus the most amazing musicianship from band members, orchestral players and instrumentalists from the far pavilions and beyond.

I'm always fascinated to move forward with the great musical adventure, still "striving to move beyond existing stagnant music forms" today! Every country around the world I visit becomes a musical inspiration, I love all forms of music from the past and I'm equally intrigued by technological musical inventions. Music is a constant universe of discovery.

I guess I'll always be that restless spirit, constantly in search of a new dimension. But alongside the joy of exploration, I finally feel at peace within. I can see why it was tough for Mum to manage me as a child, as I was always struggling to break free of any remotely constraining situation, even if it was just a trip on a tube train! 1950s Pimlico seemed to be constantly walling me in. It was as if I was a child version of the character in The Truman Show movie, sensing that there was a big cosmos beyond the confines of my concrete world, and briefly experiencing it in Canada. I still live in London, but it's a transformed world. I remain close to the river, but in a greener spot, a stone's throw from Eel Pie Island where I first fell in love with Chicago Blues.

Music became my passport to the wider sphere. I guess I was destined to be "A Genesis". I'll always be grateful to the band. Genesis gave me the chance I needed to perfect my craft, to establish myself as a musician, exposure to a whole range of musical visions and to travel the world. I continue to live with the band's legacy to this day. Then going it alone was another huge adventure with a steep learning curve. But it did enable me to come into my own. I've always pitted myself against the elements, but it's well worth discovering more and more wonderful sounds in that universe of infinite possibility.

Nowadays, I'm celebrating the Genesis music I truly love, alongside solo albums which I think are my best. I feel I've arrived with my own work, whilst maintaining a link with what was of true value from the past. I'm proud to be "a Genesis" now, in the real sense of the word. The Genesis music will always be in my soul. At the same time, all the multicoloured ducks on the wall are flying in formation to create the music I always dreamed of.

With Jo I have both a strong reciprocal working relationship and a partner who encourages me every inch of the way, with consistent and powerful love between us. We're both quickened by the feeling that we can take on anything and metaphorically fly together. That once lonely frightened child is now fulfilled, constantly in love and able to take his spaceship whenever he wants with his girl at his side to the farthest reaches of space and time… and wherever we are, we feel at home.

I have finally found home.

EPILOGUE

Life through lockdown and beyond

Many thanks to everyone who has so far responded so positively to this book. Yes, my childhood world was a tad Dickensian. 1950s London was indeed a dangerous place, acrid smoke snaking from every chimney, train engine and doorway, with bombsites scarring every street and artful dodgers lurking around every corner. The 1960s exploded in a new way, as if someone had upended the paintbox with weird and wonderful music, sweeping away the old world in a tidal wave of innovation. A few years on, my time with Genesis was both challenging and transformative. My solo career, hard on the heels of that success, gave a chance to express all those ideas which had been bubbling under the surface.

Some people have asked why I didn't flesh out the years 1987 – 2007 in more detail. In that chapter I focussed on memorable events, but it was hard to give a continuous picture. My career felt like swimming uphill and it was an emotionally traumatic period for me as well. A court order precludes me from discussing events which occurred over the years culminating in my divorce from Kim Poor, plus also for legal reasons I did not go into the related court proceedings.

Since 2010, with a brilliant partnership and a fantastic team, my life both personally and professionally has taken off like a phoenix in full flight. This year Jo and I are looking forward to celebrating our tenth wedding anniversary. Time flies when so many of your dreams come true...

It's been several months since my book first hit the online stores. A year ago when I wrote my final missives, we were in Lockdown. In the same position even now, here are some additional utterances...

At least, with the vaccine finally being rolled out, we should be able to get back on the road soon. I realise there will be certain changes. Reflecting on the 1970s, I often had to strip naked at customs. Suspicion was the norm. Unless an equable solution is negotiated between our government and the EU, this could now happen again. Post-Brexit, touring in Europe is likely to once more be a minefield, with visas, carnets (equipment manifests) etc for each country and for each person. I remember when some customs officials wanted to take apart each screw from every fuzz box. Imagine how long that can take with a large truck full of equipment. Sometimes we even missed shows because of this. Particularly at a time when the pandemic is wreaking long term havoc, the world really does need to pull together to beat the common enemy, Covid-19 and its repercussions. But whatever the obstacles, I'll ensure I still get out there and play to everyone as soon as possible – There is light at the end of the Chunnel!

My recent album, *Under A Mediterranean Sky*, also flies in the face of nationalism and the pandemic. It celebrates all those spectacular places around the Med, where the three continents of Europe, Asia and Africa converge. It's a virtual journey to a region of vibrant colour... the perfect virtual Lockdown sojourn. In spirit, I'm a lover of the Med with my nomadic life, contemplating a hotter sun with olive groves and grapes ripening under that gorgeous sky, yielding fruits fit for a king. When I'm in the Med I start to hear music, whether it's staring down over the balustrades from the overlook of an Italian hilltop town, or when I'm watching Spanish gypsies playing and dancing as if they were giving a show which their very lives depend on. From the sumptuous water gardens of the Alhambra in Spain to the extraordinary fountains of the Villa D'Este in Italy, I find endless inspiration. I'm not the only musician who feels this. We all in Genesis celebrated the wonder of water in The Fountain Of Salmacis, Lamia and Ripples. Musical cascades bring mythological sculptures to life in Respighi's Fountains of Rome and shimmering arpeggios perfectly evoke rising and falling water in Rodrigo's *Concierto de Aranjuez*... Music which hit me with the force of a thousand waterfalls.

Many people have been intrigued the way *Under A Mediterranean Sky* has virtually taken them to all those beautiful places at a time when it's incredibly difficult and dangerous to actually travel. Even stepping outside your front door can be lethal... There's hardly a family this hasn't impacted upon in the entire world. Throughout this bastard of a time, I've been concerned about the crew, all of whom were suddenly left without a job. We've sold t-shirts, masks and personalised lyrics to raise money for them and soften the blow.

Sixty shows were cancelled on us and we had to reschedule them all. During the Spring Lockdown, I put out sixty videos to help keep up the morale of fans. As soon as I was able to record again, Roger King and I put together the acoustic album, followed by other waxings, soon to be released as a new rock album. This became a lifeline… We worked in a fever throughout every day into evenings right up to late November when I had an operation to remove a kidney cyst, which thankfully I've now recovered from. As I write, we plan to resume recording as soon as Lockdown relaxes. In the meantime, Jo and I are working on many ideas which will spring out of the rocking musical box ASAP!

Speaking of musical boxes, it's always nice to connect with several of the Genesis guys. Recently, I've been in touch with Pete, Phil, Ant Phillips and Richard MacPhail, and I had a nice message in a Christmas card from Tony and wife Margaret. It's now over fifty years since I first played with the band. Extraordinary to think that so much time has passed by. We still all celebrate the music in our own ways today, and I'm looking forward to bringing my Seconds Out & More show to audiences as soon as everything opens up again this year…

The music goes on in my dreams and in my waking life, sometimes obsessively so, but like I've said before, the devil is in the detail. You could call this an addiction, but it's also an expression of love and it's the air that Jo and I breathe together. Can't wait to be playing with the band again on the road. Our Odyssey continues…

Index

Song titles in single quotation marks; albums, films, TV shows and literary titles in italics.

Index

Index

199

Index

Mosley, Ian 139

Mozart, Wolfgang Amadeus 93

Mulford, Phil 164

Murdoch, Rupert 113

Murphy, Frank 63

Muses, the 162

'Musical Box, The' 72, 74, 77, 82

Musique Concrete 66

Nice, The 55

Nightingale, Anne 132

Night Siren, The 181, 183

NME 136

'Nomads' 169

'Not Fade Away' 50

'Now That The Buffalo's Gone' 53

Nursery Cryme 73-74, 76, 78, 95

Nursery Cryme Tour 78

Ode to Joy 85

'Oh Susanna' 11

Oldfield, Mike 107

Oldfield, Sally 107

Old Scotland Yard 57

Oliver 67

Oliver Twist 14, 27

Olympia, Paris 87

One Day in the Life of Ivan Denisovich 135

'On the Turning Away' 54

Orpheus 162

Orwell, George 9

O'Toole, Gary 164, 171

Out of the Tunnel's Mouth 170-171, 175

'Overnight Sleeper' 138

Page, Jimmy 96

Pallai, Péter 34

Palmer, Freddy 165

Pearce, Harry 173

Peck, Gregory 5

Peter Gabriel III 178

Phillips, Anthony 69, 173, 178, 190

Phish 177

Piaf, Edith 87

Piano Concerto in B Flat Minor
(Tchaikovsky) 38

'Pines of Rome' 81, 179

Pink Floyd 15, 54-55, 85, 134

Pinocchio 15, 28

'Pipeline' 30

Piper Club, Rome 82

Pizza Express, Fulham Road 50, 84

Plant, Robert 96

Plato 116

Please Don't Touch 116, 118, 125-128,
131, 178

'Please Don't Touch' 116, 125, 132

Podola, Günther 31

Poe, Edgar Allen 72

Polanski, Roman 143

Poldark 144

Pomeroy, Lee 175

Poor, Kim 102, 138, 169-170, 187

Pretenders, The 135

Price, Vincent 100

Prog 121, 175

Putney High School for Girls 41

Quant, Mary 51

Queen (group) 52, 154

Queen Elizabeth II 8

Quiet World 59-60

Index

A Genesis In My Bed